Behaviour Can Change

E. V. S. Westmacott and R. J. Cameron

Globe Education

ISBN 0333 29608 7

First Published 1981 by
GLOBE EDUCATION,
a division of Macmillan Education Ltd,
Houndmills, Basingstoke, Hampshire RG21 2XS

Filmset by Vantage Photosetting Co. Ltd,
Southampton and London

Printed in Hong Kong.

Contents

To Susie, Helen and Robert
who are still learning.

Not forgetting, of course,
our parents who taught us.

Acknowledgements

Thanks are due to our friends and colleagues with whom we have worked and learned. We should like to particularly acknowledge the contributions of R. Stratford and A. Gale, Department of Psychology at Southampton University, the Wessex Health Care Evaluation Research Team, Winchester and Chelfham Mill School, Devon.

Thanks are due to S. Crawford-Hill and all those who have helped with the manuscript including P. O'Sullivan, L. Smith and D. Mahoney who read the manuscript and suggested improvements. Most of all we are indebted to those parents and teachers with whom we have worked in the past and who have clearly shown us that, given a modicum of help, they could achieve marvellous results with the children in their care.

E.V.S.W.
R.J.C.

Prologue

Parents, teachers, child care staff, playgroup staff and child minders all share one very important and often overlooked feature: they spend considerable periods of time in *direct contact* with children. This means that when behaviour problems arise, direct contact people are often in a position to have the time, the detailed information and the vested interest to change the behaviour of the children concerned.

Professional people from the caring agencies like Health, Social Services and Education have long agreed that when problems do arise, it is vital to involve parents, teachers and others as *partners* in tackling these problems. Parents can be helped by learning more effective skills for working with their children. So can teachers, child care staff, playgroup staff and child minders!

The purpose of this book is to go even further and help direct contact personnel to become their own *experts* on many occasions. Some behaviour problems may indeed be complicated and need the careful diagnosis and treatment recommendations of a professional expert, but many problems which people complain about may only require the application of a simple effective strategy. *Behaviour Can Change* offers a carefully prepared framework for tackling behaviour problems. If followed, it will enable parents, teachers and others to arrive at a strategy for self help.

R. J. CAMERON

Many Roads Lead to Rome

1

Changing behaviour
The functional approach

There may be someone in your family who does things the rest of you wish he did not, or who will not behave in the way everyone wants. You may have decided to grit your teeth and accept him the way he is, believing his behaviour is 'part of his nature' and, therefore, unchangeable. Perhaps the person in question behaves just like your wife or husband, or aunt, or a great grandparent. You and the rest of your family may be hoping he will 'grow out of it' in time, or you may believe he cannot change. Sometimes parents become so convinced that their children are hopeless that they even want to send them away from the family!

Most people think it is difficult to change other people's behaviour but behaviour can be changed deliberately. These pages contain a simple formula. Use it whenever you want to teach someone anything new. Use it when you want to change bad behaviour for good.

Until now, parents and teachers who have wanted to change the behaviour of others have usually needed to visit psychologists or other experts to learn these techniques. We are offering you a system which will enable you to deal directly with problem behaviour. Since this book is written primarily for parents and teachers we will be concentrating on dealing with problem behaviour exhibited by children. However, the techniques we mention have been successfully used many times over the past decade to change the behaviour of adults as well.

What do we mean by behaviour? Why do we say our approach is more useful to you than other methods?

What is behaviour?

Usually when people use the word behaviour, it is coupled with an adjective like 'good' or 'bad'. *When we use the term 'behaviour' it refers to any single observable action.* Simple activities like eating, sleeping, smiling, talking, walking, shopping or sitting are behaviours. Normally we take most of these behaviours for granted and do not notice where one behaviour ends and the other begins.

Daily life is an interlocking series of behaviours. Each melts into the next as people share activities, break away to do things on their own, are distracted by interesting radio or television programmes, or have to keep other appointments. Even if someone begins a day with an organised plan and a 'do list' by teatime something will have been added or been overlooked. Living is behaving!

Accepting life as though each of us is acting our way through a non-ending play is fine until someone wants to change something about their own or someone else's behaviour pattern. At that point we need the skill of isolating behaviours, recognising each tiny activity in its separateness as a behaviour.

Seeing behaviour clearly

How easy it is to see individual behaviours in isolation in a film and how difficult it is in real life!

In a film the director has complete control of events. He interlocks scenes so that each will make it more likely that a particular event will occur later. The viewer can begin to predict what will happen. Many claim great pleasure from seeing a film and watching for clues in order to predict future events. That is why cinema enthusiasts watch complex films like Hitchcock's *Psycho* repeatedly, each time trying to fit the jigsaw puzzle together more accurately.

The director can isolate a behaviour and freeze it for seconds on the screen while his audience takes in a desired clue or piece of information. As he films each scene he sees exactly how the actor behaves, the way he moves or speaks and the effect that this has on others in the scene. The director can re-shoot, re-write or even leave whole chunks of action on the cutting room floor to retain the precise behaviour that he needs to make his story work. By clever use of camera angles and cuts in action it is relatively easy for him to focus attention on certain behaviours to the exclusion of others.

During a film the audience begins to anticipate what will happen next. Its attention is concentrated on little cues for behaviour. Imagine a typical western, the scene is the cattle town's saloon full of cowboys drinking. The good guy (usually distinguishable by a white hat) is innocently playing cards. We hear the music quicken and the camera picks up a pair of desert-scuffed boots striding across the sand. The camera cuts to a hand on the swing doors and pans back to reveal the villain (sometimes wearing a black hat) carrying a gun. He pauses in the doorway. The camera cuts to our hero who raises his eyes from his cards and coolly surveys the intruder. By this point everyone has guessed that there is going to be a confrontation, a gun fight, or will the drunken sheriff arrive in time?

In the real world it is much more difficult to identify behaviours. Each person sees only a part of a situation. It is particularly hard to see ourselves objectively. We know when we move or speak but we cannot gauge precisely how these behaviours affect others. We receive feedback in the form of reactions from others as they smile, reply, or even turn away in response. We cannot see ourselves and others at the same moment except perhaps on a video-tape or film. So it is difficult to identify precisely which of our actions caused a particular response.

Unless we are particularly alert and observant it is easy to overlook those clues in real life. Mum is in the kitchen cooking supper in a peaceful mood when in walks her husband. She does not see the weary way in which he throws his newspaper on the table or hear his sigh of relief as he begins to sit down. She is concentrating on something on the hob and hears a scream from upstairs. She has a choice of either stopping what she is doing at a critical moment or asking her husband to go and investigate. Had she picked up those two little clues that her husband was tired and needing a little time of peace and quiet in which to recharge his batteries she would probably choose the former. As she has not she asks him to go upstairs. He snaps back and now she has a husband who is being unpleasant, a child crying and a saucepan boiling over. Her peace is a thing of the past.

If both the husband and wife in this little scenario had been able to stand back and watch the scene unfold, they might have been able to see their behaviours as building the eventual row. Unfortunately, the wife in this case was so involved in her cooking that she was oblivious to the way her behaviour was affecting her husband. While his use of home as a re-charging point created a situation which easily erupted.

The most important point about this little domestic scene is that a visitor who had observed the events unfold could have predicted the eventual row as easily as anyone who viewed the film of the saloon scene in the previous example. It is not easy to stand back and see how our behaviour affects others.

Often when people see themselves on film for the first time they register surprise at the sound of their voices or the way that they move. Some people say their view of themselves changes after listening to a tape or watching a video, and remark that the impression they had of themselves previously now seems inaccurate. Some people compare the experience to the effects of looking in a distorting mirror at a fairground.

The fact that we do see our own behaviour unclearly may be one of the reasons why a 'bad behaviour' is rarely seen as a problem by the person who has behaved 'badly'. It is other people who cannot tolerate a particular behaviour who say it is 'bad' or 'a problem'. In one family a high level of noise may be accepted. Their youngest son's habit of letting out a high pitch squeal of pleasure every time he finishes an activity is not considered a problem. But when he goes to school or to stay with his quietest aunt, squawks can swiftly become described as most disturbing behaviour.

Even when a group agrees that someone's behaviour has become a problem, the offender may be blissfully unaware of what he is doing or how annoying it is to others. However inadequately we see our own behaviour and its effect on others, we are only too aware of the way our friends' or our family's behaviours impinge on our lives. It is not surprising, therefore, that at some time everybody tries to change someone else's behaviour in a direction which they think will be better for the person or for everyone else concerned.

The key idea behind this book

If you want to change someone else's behaviour, you must define it and be clear about what it is you want to change. However, you will not stop someone from being persistently late for appointments, or smoking too heavily, or running up large overdrafts by just drawing his attention to the habit. A much closer analysis of the ABC of behaviour is necessary. Behaviours which we wish to change are either the ones which do not occur frequently enough or those which happen with such persistence that our lives are made uncomfortable. But the person who is guilty of the behaviour is often not aware of the effect of those bits of behaviour because, for him, they are just a very small part of the total behaviours which make up his everyday life.

The behaviour of which people complain must be broken down into its individual components and examined against the background in which it occurs. It must be established what makes it possible for it to occur repeatedly. *Know your ABC of behaviour; A stands for the antecedents, or events which occurred before the behaviour. B is for the background in which the behaviour occurred. C is for the consequences (the events which occurred after the behaviour).*

ANTECEDENTS ⟶ BACKGROUND ⟶ BEHAVIOUR ⟶ CONSEQUENCES
    A   B   C

A functional approach

The first thing that is different about the way we tackle problem behaviours is that results come swiftly. No agonising years of therapy, no weekly visits to the friendly neighbourhood psychologist. We offer a short term effective formula which you can operate successfully *if you stick to the rules.*

The second way in which our approach is different is that it concentrates on the specific behaviour problem. A famous psychologist, B. F. Skinner,[1] suggested that any person can be said to have a problem when he is unable in a particular situation to make an appropriate response.

A person can be said to have a problem when he is
unable to make an appropriate response

[1] Skinner, B. F. *About Behaviourism* (Jonathan Cape, 1974).

The implication of that statement is that one behaviour can be both 'good' or 'bad'. For instance, would anyone agree that screaming in a crowded supermarket, a church or a restaurant is a good way to behave? Yet who would find fault with someone screaming to draw attention to a child running in front of a car, a house erupting into flames, or a dog falling into a weir? Whether the behaviour is 'good' or 'bad' usually depends on the context.

The trick about changing a behaviour is to (a) isolate the behaviour (b) find the various factors which allow it to occur (or prevent it from occurring) in the first place (c) establish what makes it possible for it to continue or decrease in the future.

When parents ask advice from members of their family, a doctor, the local wise woman or their next door neighbour about their children's problem behaviour, they ask precise questions. "How", they might say, "do I stop Johnny lying/or punching/or stealing/or running away?" "What can I do", they might ask, "to get him to do his homework/or talk to me/or sleep through the night/or eat his food with a knife and fork?"

Often the answer will come in a form of a universal method which has been known to work in the past but, which may or may not be appropriate in that parent's particular circumstances. Advice may be given like, "Leave him alone, he'll soon grow out of it", or "Have you tried stopping her pocket money", or "You have to be firm with him – don't take any nonsense".

The best way to solve any problem is through a functional approach. Using a functional approach means analysing all the influences exerted by the events which occurred *before*, *during* and *after* the problem behaviour.

This approach stems from the assumption that *a person behaves in a certain way because he has been taught to behave in that way or because he has not been taught to behave differently.* In short, almost all behaviour is learned. A child learns that if he eats his food his parents are pleased. A child learns that if he pulls the dog's tail he is growled at and may be bitten. Thus one behaviour he repeats often and the other little if at all. His parents have taught him by their behaviour what they desire from him. So has the dog!

It's a new approach

Not all psychologists adopt a functional approach. To be honest, we did not until we had been working as psychologists long enough to discover that of all the techniques available to us this was the most

A person behaves in a certain way because he has
been taught or because he has not been taught to
behave differently

effective. Like so many other psychologists we carried around several attaché cases filled with specialist tests to measure intelligence, personality factors, physical skills and the strength of family relationships. We used to be interested in examining *why* a child behaved in the way he did. Our efforts were therefore directed towards *explaining* and *interpreting* behaviour and hoping that by so doing we were helping parents to 'understand' their children's problems.

In fact our efforts were sometimes successful. The families we worked with occasionally reported that 'family stresses were reduced' or that as parents they were able to 'cope better'. But the outstanding feature of our style of practice then was that the more concrete, tangible and observable problems were to an extent ignored.

When asking for our advice, doctors, parents or teachers who had referred children were apt to make blanket statements about the problems these children posed. Thus a lot of initial interview time was spent trying to discover what was the problem. It is a common belief that if a person is given 'insight' or in other words told *why* he does something he will be able to change his own behaviour. Regrettably our experience as well as any review of scientific research papers yields little evidence, other than anecdotal, to suggest that this statement is true.

So before we developed the functional approach we now use, we would spend hours using our tests and speculating with all the people involved about the reasons *why* children were exhibiting behaviour problems. Sometimes we ended up very dissatisfied with the results of these interviews since one thing we noticed was that people to whom we had given 'insight explanations' sometimes used our explanation as a reason for continuing the problem behaviour or even repeating it more frequently!

Have you heard remarks like, "I shall continue to smoke cigarettes because as a child I was deprived and lacked appropriate oral gratification". Or read of a barrister pleading, "M'lud, the evidence suggests that the defendant is repeatedly involved in these squalid and sordid episodes because he cannot control his aggressive personality". Or giggled at the classic, "I know I'm paranoid – that doesn't mean that people are not getting at me".

There is a marked difference in the way we tackle problems now than when we were playing at explaining what was going on 'inside somebody's head'.

We will give an example; a common problem parents complain about is the child who will not go to bed and who even when in bed creeps downstairs with the flimsiest excuse. In the old days we would have amassed a considerable amount of information about the family group and how the members of the family related to each other. The emotional reactions, desires, aspirations of the parents and all the children would have been minutely examined. At the end of the session we would produce explanations which might demonstrate that the child was feeling 'insecure' and looking for 'reassurance'. Or perhaps we would find that 'jealousy' of the relationship of a brother and sister with the parents was causing problems. Perhaps the family was a reconstituted group of two second families and we might have suggested that the child was 'not sure of his position in the group' and had become 'attention seeking'.

The parents would leave such a session possibly feeling more comfortable about the complained of behaviour *but not necessarily with a clear plan of how to change it.* Sometimes, of course, very clear and explicit plans were laid and the parents would go away and report later on their success.

If we were now faced with this 'creeping downstairs problem' we would use a functional approach and concentrate our attention on the actual behaviour itself. Thus questions like the following would be asked: "Does he go to bed the same time every night?" "Is there a system at bed time?" "Do you read him a story?" "Does he have a bath?" "Who usually tucks him into bed?" "Do you both kiss him goodnight?" The answers to these questions build up a picture of the events which occur before the 'getting up' and 'coming downstairs' behaviour. These are the *antecedents* in the ABC of behaviour.

Secondly, questions which centred on the behaviour itself and the background against which it occurred would be asked: "Who is downstairs at these times?" "Do either of you go out in the evening?" "Is his elder sister downstairs?" "Does it happen more often when you have guests in the house?" and "Are the lights on upstairs?" Such questions help us to see more clearly the *background* or setting within which the behaviour occurred.

Finally the reactions of the family when the child appears, the *consequences* in the ABC would be examined: "What do you do when he appears on the stairs?" "Do you take him straight downstairs again?" "Do you allow him to stay upstairs until he stops whining?" "Does his sister ever do anything to help?"

The ABC of behaviour is designed to find out how the child learned the behaviour of coming downstairs and the answers would be used to help the child to *unlearn* this behaviour. A behaviour occurs because of the balance between the antecedents, the background and the consequences. Thus to change behaviour the balance between these three needs to be altered.

Our functional approach concentrates on helping people to overcome problems. Since opting for the methods you will find outlined in this book we have successfully helped several hundred people to change their behaviour. This means a reduction in the number of times those people acted in a way which made their own lives or the lives of those around them uncomfortable or, conversely, it means that we have helped people to increase those behaviours which everyone around them agreed to be desirable. Most important of all we have taught people that *behaviour can change.*

It really is a better way

It is fun solving problems through a functional approach because so often the analysis of a situation enables a swift end to a lifetime's habit which has become quite destructive. One such case was a young naval midshipman.

He wanted to become a navigation officer. It was not going well for him, he had made many errors and his senior officers were questioning whether he was intelligent enough for the job. He appeared incompetent and before dropping him from his course, it was arranged that he should see a psychologist.

Fortunately for him, he saw a psychologist who used a functional approach. The interview began with the completion of an intelligence test which his superiors had requested and which showed that the man was of well above average ability. The psychologist began probing the situation in which the midshipman had been incompetent. He swiftly discovered one common denominator. In each case the man had had to distinguish port and starboard and had failed to do so! It may not matter too much when driving a car if your passenger says left when meaning right and you take the wrong turning. When bringing a ship into harbour saying port when you mean starboard could cause a major catastrophe.

If the interviewing psychologist had been 'playing the explanations game' he could have told the young man he had an 'emotional blockage' or even a 'confidence problem'. Such a psychologist might also have produced an elaborate explanation relating this to historical supposition like the way in which the young man was breast fed or even the angle at which he lay in the womb. A less fanciful explanation might have been given if the 'explaining' psychologist had discovered that when the midshipman was in his first year at school he had broken his right arm and had been faced with the problem of using his left hand to write. Either of the above explanations might have made it easier for him to accept why he experienced confusion, but it is doubtful if they would have helped him to overcome his problem.

What the functional psychologist did in fact was almost ridiculously simple. He suggested that the midshipman sewed a large button inside each of his right-hand trouser pockets. By feeling in his pockets he could instantly establish which side was 'right'. From then on the midshipman could be seen nonchalently standing hands in pockets correctly identifying port and starboard! Reassured by the results of the IQ test which had been requested his superiors were prepared to give him another chance and using the button strategy over the next few weeks he began to be more successful. The psychologist concerned had the satisfaction of seeing positive results and improvements from a very simple intervention.

This is how the functional psychologist arrived at his ingenious intervention. He decided that since it would be very difficult to change either the background in which the problem behaviour occurred or the consequences of the behaviour, the only events left to change were the antecedents. He helped the young midshipman to change his behaviour before he acted. Previously he had been fussing around, or pacing up and down desperately trying to work out which direction was starboard. Now those antecedents changed to feeling in his pockets in order to correctly identify port or starboard.

The changes suggested by the psychologist in ABC terms are shown below:

Table 1   Events Surrounding Behaviour

Events Surrounding Behaviour	From	To
A (antecedents)	fussing, pacing up and down and worrying about getting answer incorrect	feeling for button in pocket and correctly identifying port or starboard
B (background)	no change	no change
C (consequences)	no change	no change

Behaviour

Antecedents　　　　　　　Background　　　　　　　Consequence

Behaviour does change

Underlying the functional approach is an assumption that a person's behaviour does not always remain the same but changes with changing circumstances. Each activity or group of behaviours, like slicing a grapefruit or preparing a meal for a dozen people, is influenced by a variety of happenings in a person's environment. Unless you happen to be a hermit or stranded on a desert island most people find that their environment is constantly changing as new events rapidly follow one another. Behaviour is continually changing too and being changed by the ebb and flow of daily experiences which include events which have occurred in the past, others taking place at that time, and often too, the person's predictions (both hopeful and fearful) of future events.

In our jigsaw diagram we show the most important elements which affect a behaviour. Here, the process has been 'frozen'. In real life this is an ongoing situation where ABC events themselves are not static but change from time to time and behaviour changes as a result.

People who wish to change behaviour need a crystal clear description of the behaviour which they wish to change and the events controlling this behaviour. Such close observation is not easy. People adapt to changing circumstances so quickly and skilfully that the events causing change can become as difficult to spot as a mosquito in a dark bedroom.

Parents and teachers do observe

Parents, teachers and other adults who spend long periods of time in direct contact with children are in a superb position to observe the problem behaviour of their children. However, their attempts can be bitty, confused and scrambled so they need help and guidance on what to observe.

Parents know more about their children than anyone else. But unfortunately because most people do not separate out behaviours but talk in blanket descriptions (e.g. "he's a little tearaway", "he's short-tempered", "he's selfish" . . .) this information is virtually unusable unless carefully sifted. A useful role played by psychologists, social workers and psychiatrists, is helping parents to use that information. Professional workers are expected to have a fund of knowledge of psychology and social behaviour which when married to the parents' knowledge of the child should provide answers to many problems, especially if a functional approach is adopted.

Just as parents and teachers are likely to know more about their children than any outsider, they are also in the best position to change problem behaviour. Parents and teachers are almost inevitably with children in a variety of settings every day: classrooms, playgrounds, supermarkets, your home, your neighbour's home, etc. Unwanted behaviour can occur in any of these places. *The most direct and effective way of dealing with problem behaviour is to help parents and teachers to acquire the necessary skills to achieve behaviour changes, in the setting in which the unwanted behaviour occurs.*

Treating behaviour out of context

Although it seems sensible to help the person in direct contact to improve his system for handling difficult behaviour, strangely enough social workers, psychiatrists and psychologists (including ourselves) believed in the past that the best way to solve problem behaviours which occurred, for example in the home, was by treating the child and parents separately.

One example with which we were involved (not to our credit) was the case of young Micky. His behaviour would have made most parents' hair stand on end. He was constantly involved in fights at school and in his neighbourhood. He stayed out late, took no notice of parents' requests to come in for meals or bedtime, did no school work unless his teacher stood immediately beside him and was facing a possible court appearance for ill-treating cats. The case was being treated by the local child guidance clinic personnel. Micky, aged nine, was described as a youngster who lacked 'internal controls' and had 'low ego strength'. The school was seen as 'containing' Micky but not 'able to provide a caring environment'. What was wrong with Micky was said to be 'inside him' and nothing to do with his immediate environment.

Since no attempt was made to analyse or focus on his acts of bad behaviour or the circumstances in which they occurred, their analysis of the situation led the clinic team to treat these problems outside the home. In fact the psychiatrist saw the boy for 'counselling' on a weekly basis while the social worker had a session of 'therapy' with the parents during which marital problems were discussed. What actually happened in the counselling and the therapy sessions is not known. Micky's behaviour continued unabated and after a stormy term in which the parents separated once and the mother was involved in a punch-up with her next door neighbour, the team agreed that Micky should leave home. A boarding school for 'maladjusted' children was

sought and it took about one term for the psychologist to make all the necessary arrangements. By that time Micky had broken into a builder's yard and had been caught by the police.

Eventually Micky went off to his new school and everyone breathed sighs of relief. The local school had a holiday atmosphere for a day or two. The parents were relaxed and ceased fighting and the first reports from the new school on Micky's behaviour were most encouraging.

So what happened when the now virtuous Micky returned home six weeks later for the holidays? He had completed a term of near perfect behaviour: no fights, no truancy, no rudeness, hard work in class and he had been picked for the school soccer team. His parents looked forward to receiving the new Micky.

For a week all was quiet. In the second week the clinic had a call from the mother asking for an urgent appointment. A few days later the mother appeared with Micky in tow. "His Dad said I was to tell you to keep him," she said belligerently. "I can't have the little devil at home no more." Protesting at the top of her voice she was ushered into the social worker's room while Micky dutifully followed the psychiatrist for his counselling session.

It is worth asking why, when a child is removed from the setting in which the problems arise, the child no longer behaves badly and, why also, when the child returns to his original environment the same old behaviour problems appear? There are probably many reasons for this frequently observed phenomenon but we would like you to consider one important one. Do *you* behave differently in different situations?

There are many household rules which are frequently told to children, e.g. "Feet off the arm chair", "No dawdling on the way home from school", or "Tea is always at five o'clock". There are also many unwritten rules which have become established by habit. Multiply all the little rules in a household and you will find many kinds of behaviour which up until now you had not even thought of as rules. Who puts the cat out at night? Who is in the bathroom first in the morning? Who has a special chair or place at a table and so on?

Sadly, 'out of context' treatment often means that a child learns a new set of rules for behaviour while he is in the new environment. Return him to the same background conditions, react in the same old way to a piece of behaviour and you will have the same problem behaviours as before.

Of course with the very small number of children who have to leave home because of the management problems which they are causing, a return home from a special school can be successful. In these cases usually the parents have been taught new skills of observing and analysing both their child's and their own behaviour during the interim period. Regrettably with the enormous pressure of work on psychiatrists, social workers and psychologists too often there is no time to teach parents enough while children are away. The techniques in this book will help to fill this gap for the small number of families who have a child at a residential special school, as well as the majority of parents who want to be able to deal effectively with one or two behaviour problems which their child exhibits at home.

Behaviour can change
Basically the whole system rests on the simple assumption that a piece of behaviour is not a static factor dependent on emotional features inside someone's head. In fact, behaviour is a dynamic event promoted, controlled and shaped by many influences and events going on in the environment, as well as factors unique to the individual like previous learning and experience.

Certain behaviours are totally dependent on the presence of other people – have you ever tried to throw a temper tantrum in an empty room? Others are controlled by environmental conditions such as the weather; ever tried suntanning in a snow storm? Some are likely to be determined by the person's experiences immediately after the behaviour. Imagine two very different behaviours; chewing and swallowing the chilli pepper from the pickle jar, or kissing a member of the opposite sex. These two behaviours are guaranteed to produce distinctly different results; one is likely never to occur again, while it is just possible that you might get hooked on repeating the other again, and again, and again!

In beginning to think about how to change your own or other people's behaviour, several aspects of behaviour have to be understood – firstly what constitutes a behaviour . . . secondly how a behaviour is learned . . . thirdly what makes it possible for a behaviour to continue . . . and finally how can we alter some of these things so as to make the behaviour change?

Repeatedly when parents and teachers begin devising strategies to teach new behaviours to children, or to help them to unlearn unpleasant habits, they discover they have to begin by changing something about *their* own behaviour which is affecting the child's behaviour.

Be warned: to change someone else's behaviour the person who desires the behaviour changed often will have to start by modifying his own behaviour.

Starting point

Begin, as we did, by trying to unlearn the conventional way of describing behaviour speculatively. It is so easy to slip into statements like "Christopher is angry with his sister", or "I think Christopher is worried about my close relationship with his sister". What do these inferences tell us? Are they even accurate? These descriptions are vague and give no indication at all of how Christopher could be made less 'worried', 'angry' or 'jealous'. Can everybody agree what is happening when Christopher is experiencing these feelings? Difficult to be sure, isn't it?

Learn to describe what you see and no more. For instance if the statement is made, "Christopher hits his sister frequently", or "Christopher tears up his sister's drawings and paintings before she can show them to me", or "Christopher cries and screams when I put his sister on my lap to read to her", the problem is immediately clear. It may well be that the behaviours so described fit into a picture which has been seen before and described as 'jealousy'. But as no one climbs inside Christopher's head who can be sure what he is feeling? Only he knows what his reactions are and for a variety of reasons he may not wish to tell.

A clear description of behaviour is the beginning of a functional approach and the starting point for changing behaviour. From a statement which describes behaviour, without speculating about inner causes, it is possible to plan to change Christopher's hitting, tearing and screaming behaviour. Then people will not complain any more. Once he is no longer showing signs of these behaviours it does not matter if you return to the 'speculation game' and say, "Christopher is no longer feeling angry, worried or jealous". For guessing another's feelings is no problem to anyone once the behaviour has returned to normal.

So what have we said so far?

The most important message we bring you is that *Behaviour Can Change* – and YOU can deliberately change your own and other people's behaviour. It took us a long time to discover that the easiest, swiftest way of helping people to deal with problem behaviour is by using a functional approach.

Now we have mastered the techniques we want to share them with you. As parents and teachers you are at the business end of the problem. Life will be a lot easier if you learn ways of dealing with your children's behaviour problems. To begin, think of each action as a separate behaviour. Remember, all behaviour has to be learned.

Each behaviour is controlled by *antecedent* events, the *background* in which it occurs and the *consequences* thereafter. *Do not forget your ABC.*

Do not be fooled into thinking someone else can take your child away, change him or her into an angel and he will stay that way once he comes home. Out of *context* treatment rarely works.

Begin by trying to observe behaviour and describe it with fine accuracy. Forget speculation and learn description!

And read the rest of this book!

2

Identifying behaviour clearly

The problem behaviours which people complain about are of two main types – excesses and deficits. (Remember, the word behaviour refers to any clearly describable action. A behaviour can be as slight as a smile or as gross as a temper tantrum.)

We see different bits of behaviour all day. Sometimes we say, "If only he would do more of that", or "If only she would always do so and so!" Others make us complain, "If only she would stop doing that", or "I wish he did that less often".

In the first instance we are referring to *behavioural deficits*, behaviours we approve of and want more of from others. In the second to *behavioural excesses*, those behaviours which irritate and annoy, because they occur too often.

This is a useful way to approach problems as we state clearly not only what the problem behaviours are, but can also say what would be happening if the problems causing complaint were solved.

If we want to change behaviour it is necessary to define the complained of behaviour precisely. Psychologists call this the 'problem behaviour'. The new behaviour we want to see instead is called the 'target behaviour'.

If a nine-month-old baby is waking up crying five or six times between midnight and six in the morning, the crying behaviour would be called the 'problem behaviour'. The parents would be able to state that their 'target behaviour' would be for the child to sleep through the night, or perhaps wake up only once during this period. Another example of a 'problem behaviour' might be a husband who spent every Sunday morning indulging his favourite sport and returning home for lunch late. The 'problem behaviour' would be his lateness for the family meal. The wife's expressed 'target behaviour' for her husband might be that he arrived promptly at one o'clock or perhaps at a quarter-to-one, in time to set the table.

The troubles caused by labelling

Identifying problem and target behaviours is not easy. It is easier to talk in general terms of behavioural deficits and excesses, as precise definition means hard work. By the time a behaviour has become a problem it has acquired overlays of other behaviours and may overlap into other situations so that isolating the problem may be difficult. Remember your ABC clarifies confused situations.

Often professionals whose job it is to help families, describe problem behaviours in neat elliptical, vague phrases such as: "John seems to have an emotional blockage somewhere", or "Mary seems to lack motivation", or "Clive has inadequate internal controls".

They may talk in equally obscure terms about what they intend to do to help, so that no one is quite sure what will happen like: "What we will do is help him to come to terms with this problem", or "We must improve his self-concept", or even "We ought to help him achieve greater insight".

At first these statements seem helpful, even comforting. It is arguably better for a parent or teacher confused by a child's behaviour to think "Aha, he's doing that because he's got an emotional blockage" than to think "Oh why does he do that . . . so often?" But what does one *do* about an emotional blockage? Does it help the person with the problem or his teachers or his parents to alleviate or stop the behaviour to know it is an 'emotional blockage'?

It may comfort parents to know that another adult, who is a social worker or a psychologist, is planning to help a shy, awkward adolescent to 'improve his self-concept'. But does anyone know from that phrase what is going to happen, or what changes there will be in the boy's behaviour?

There are numerous reasons why we all talk in these obscure ways about problem behaviour. Often there may be a *number* of behaviours being complained of, and there is a temptation to lump the whole ragbag under one label. It is simple to say "He's undisciplined" when we mean he never does what people ask him to do, he dresses untidily,

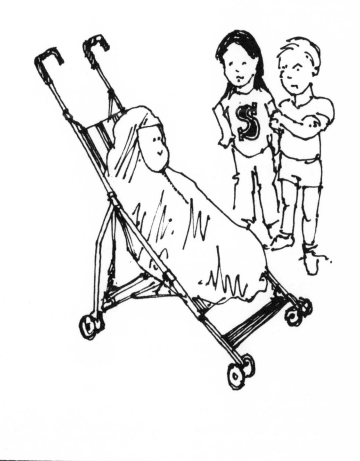

his books are in a mess, he's late for class, he giggles at inappropriate times, spends his pocket money within five minutes of receiving it and has to ask for more during the week, throws his bicycle against the wall or on the ground and forgets to put the mower back in the garden shed. It takes less time to use one word like 'undisciplined' and assume everyone understands.

The trouble is such labels can hide the problem behaviour. They discourage close and detailed examination of what the person actually does or does not do. This temptation to shorthand experience should be avoided at all costs. Far better to list each and every separate problem behaviour than to use one word which fools us into thinking it apt to cover all the behaviours.

The people who use labels perhaps more than any other group are the 'professionals'. Psychologists like us who have labels for everything from nose picking to utter stillness. Doctors who use Greek words to bunch together symptoms of diseases. Psychiatrists who have a vast range of labels like schizophrenia, mania, dementia and subconscious motivation. Social workers who like the rest of us share some labels and have some all of their own. It is understandable how we developed so many labels. All these types of 'professional workers' have been trained to *explain* behaviour.

The influence on modern psychology of people like Freud, Jung and Adler has been considerable. Freud was one of the first to suggest a link between problems in childhood, adolescence or adulthood with events which occurred earlier in a person's life. He claimed that an event momentous to the person at the time of occurrence could become part of the unconscious life of a person, still affecting behaviour many months, years or decades later while the person was quite unaware of this effect. He produced hundreds of labels to describe the behaviours he deduced were occurring like fixated development, ego, id and superego, anal personality. Jung and Adler added a few more.

Later work by such people as Bowlby, who investigated the effects of maternal deprivation (there's another of those labels!) and Burt who studied the similarities and differences between children, shaped thought towards *causes* of behaviour rather than *solutions*.

There was and is so much to observe, quantify and qualify about human behaviour that the 'why' and 'how' questions are fascinating. The answers may lead to changes in child rearing practices, or education, or may just start whole new areas of research. But the questions and answers set as they are mostly in jargon inevitably give rise to commonly used labels which attempt to describe the problem *and* ascribe a cause for it like 'emotionally disturbed', 'immature personality', or 'developmental delay'. On close examination these phrases which glide off the tongue with unsuspected ease do not convey any precise information at all. It does not matter if the listener is a psychologist, a parent, a teacher, a dustman or a ship's captain because any label can be interpreted in many different ways.

What's that?

Here is a list of labels we often hear our colleagues using to describe behavioural deficits and excesses. We have used most of them ourselves in the past.

1 low intelligence
2 hyperkinetic
3 unsettled home background
4 suffers from dyslexia
5 lack of motor co-ordination
6 inadequate attention span
7 poor self-image
8 lack of motivation
9 visual and auditory perceptual problems
10 inability to cope with abstract symbols
11 impoverished intellectual climate in the home.

How tempting it is to look at these labels and think, "I know what they mean". Look again. Take 'hyperkinetic', what does this word mean?

It is not possible to describe exactly what someone would be doing from the word 'hyperkinetic'. They might be doing any or all of the following – jumping up and down on the spot, constantly moving around the room at a fast walk, bouncing a large football, not sleeping for more than two hours in twenty-four, not able to go to sleep until very late, unable to stop talking and touching people simultaneously, often seen fiddling with tiny items like worry beads, unable to sit in a chair for longer than thirty seconds without bouncing up and down or repeatedly walking from one side of the room to the other, touching the wall and tracking off to the other side . . .

Any of these behaviours repeated with a high enough frequency might lead to a description of the child as 'hyperkinetic'. There are many other behaviours not mentioned which could cause the use of the same label. The word 'hyperkinetic' does not tell us *which behaviours* or *how* or *when* or *for how long*. It is a word of description masquerading as an explanation. In addition the word does not give us any information about what we should do to stop or change the condition and behaviour of the person with the problem.

Meet the 'fuzzies'

R. F. Mager in his amusing book *Goal Analysis*[2] describes all these labels as 'fuzzies'. *Fuzzies are unclear, imprecise and frequently ambiguous statements used to describe problems.* The use of a fuzzy to describe behavioural excesses and deficits can lead to a multitude of difficulties for the labeller and the labelled alike. Firstly, it is difficult to see what the problem is when it is described by a fuzzy. Secondly, it is difficult to see what to do to overcome or alleviate the problem. Thirdly, although it has been suggested fuzzies are a kind of professional shorthand which enable psychiatrists, doctors, nurses, psychologists and others to communicate clearly with one another, this would appear to be the case in only rare instances. In fact professionals spend hours, months and possibly years arguing over labels. They even write articles, books and hold seminars to try to define their own jargon. Finally, when problems are described by a fuzzy, everybody involved including the professional worker may find it a hard task to see how the recommended treatment relates to the problem as originally described. The cartoons overleaf expand these four points.

Unfortunately these vague, imprecise and frequently ambiguous statements about a problem are commonly used and right now there certainly seem to be a lot of fuzzies around.

Performances are useful

On the other hand, if we describe a *problem behaviour in clear, precise and non-ambiguous terms* we have got what Mager calls a 'performance'.

Switching descriptions of behavioural excesses and deficits into talk of performances is like shining a powerful searchlight into a dark night. Suddenly the speaker and the listener can see the behaviour illuminated in words which leave no doubt in either's mind what is happening when the problem behaviour occurs.

[2] Mager R. F. *Goal Analysis* (Fearon Publishers, 1974).

Looking through case files we have selected some fuzzies used by teachers and parents to describe their children's problem behaviour and the performances to which they related:

Fuzzy	Performance
"She is a filthy feeder"	Cannot raise spoon from plate to mouth without spilling food.
"He's always blabbering"	Talks aloud when left alone by Mum.
"He's disruptive"	Shouts out loudly when the teacher talks to another child.
"He won't take his punishment like a man"	After a reprimand he hits mother or younger sister.
"He lacks motor co-ordination"	He could run, jump, climb and balance as well as the rest in his class but he could not catch a tennis ball with one hand.
"She's numerically backward"	Could count aloud 1–10 but could not write those numbers in the correct sequence.
"His play is egocentric"	Kicked, shouted and screamed if denied the first choice of available toys.
"She can't concentrate"	She would work for no more than three minutes before leaving her seat or talking to her next door neighbour.
"I can't leave her with her younger brother to play"	She bit her younger brother between 30–40 times a day.
"He won't eat nicely"	When given his food on one specific dark green plate he up-ended his food on the floor.

Some of these fuzzies can be interpreted in colourful ways. The performance statements into which these fuzzies eventually were translated are precise and leave no room for interpretation other than factual. A complete stranger, a visitor, your next door neighbour or even the Man from Mars would know from those statements what was happening when these problem behaviours occurred. Any two people can agree what they would see when a child shouted loudly as the

COME OFF IT!
YOU LOOK O.K.
TO ME!

O.K. BUT WHAT'S
HE GOING TO DO
ABOUT IT THEN?

HUH! THAT OTHER BLOKE
SAID SOMETHING COMPLETELY
DIFFERENT!

WHAT YOU NEED IS
A GOOD TASTE OF THE
SLIPPER, MY LAD!

teacher talked, or every time when the most delectable morsels were placed on a dark green plate a certain child up-ended the food on the floor.

Could any two people agree exactly what they would see happening when a child was exhibiting the behaviour described by the fuzzies 'disruptive' or 'not eating nicely'?

Translating fuzzies into performances enables all involved to pin-point the problem behaviour. It is only a primary step in beginning to search for a strategy to make behaviour change (more on that subject later). In the performances listed above few of them are total statements which could lead to an intervention or strategy to produce change. More information is required before that can occur but the performances do highlight the behavioural deficit or excess of which the parent or teacher complained.

Fortunately it is a relatively easy task to turn a fuzzy into a performance. All the enquirer has to say is "Exactly what would I see happening when Fred was being (insert fuzzy of your choice)?" This usually has the effect of making the person, who used the fuzzy in the first place, express surprise that you have not understood. But then they start describing the problem behaviour as a performance!

Spotting fuzzies

It is sometimes quite difficult to identify immediately whether a statement made about a problem behaviour is a fuzzy or a performance. Some fuzzies look like performances. Fortunately, there are two strategies which allow us to discriminate between fuzzies and performances.

The first strategy is to examine the *verb* occurring in the statement about the problem. Some words are open to many interpretations and when these occur in any statement relating to a problem behaviour, the chances are high you are being faced with a red-hot fuzzy.

A non-inclusive list of these words is as follows:

to know	to enjoy
to understand	to behave
to appreciate	to believe
to grasp the significance of	to gain insight into
to come to terms with	to be aware of.

If these words are accompanied by adverbs such as 'fundamentally', 'passionately', 'really', 'infinitely', or 'interestingly', almost certainly the statement is a fuzzy.

Conversely there are many words which are open to fewer interpretation such as:

to write	to name
to recite	to stand
to identify	to feed self
to say aloud	to put on
to select	to point.

If these words or phrases are used to describe a problem the person is far more likely to be making a statement about a performance.

Hi Dad!

Even using this strategy it is still possible for some fuzzies to masquerade as performances and the second strategy is a tougher test through which few fuzzies can pass undetected. Mager refers to this test as the 'Hi, Dad test' and it is applied as follows: Before any statement about a problem insert the words "Hi, Dad, come and watch me . . .". If Dad has any difficulty in seeing exactly what is happening, the statement is a fuzzy. To use the cartoons on pages 28 and 29 as an example this would yield "Hi, Dad, come and watch me suffering from an intermittent neurological impairment". Most Dads would have the greatest difficulty seeing their sons doing just that.

If these two strategies are used properly any statement about a behaviour should be exposed for what it is, a fuzzy or a performance. To be able to exercise this skill at will is the first tool required in the serious business of changing behaviour.

Once those comments about behaviour deficits and excesses can be changed from wistful statements like "I wish he would do that more often", or "Gosh, how I wish Annie did less of that" into clear performances you can begin working towards change.

Try playing HUNT THE FUZZY. It would be nice if you scored eight out of ten. Check your rating on page **33**.

Hunt the fuzzy

Remember how to spot 'fuzzies'? Just to help, ask yourself:

A Is the verb open to many interpretations or not?

B Will the statement pass the 'Hi, Dad test'?

Please underline the following statements if you think they are 'fuzzies' or 'performances'.

1 Wayne will stop turning the knobs of the gas cooker to the 'on' position.

                                                        fuzzy/performance

2 Sally will begin to appreciate the dangers of electricity.

                                                        fuzzy/performance

3 Tina's parents need to be helped to create a home environment which is conducive to the well-being of all their children.

                                                        fuzzy/performance

4 After being sufficiently stimulated by the class teacher, Rebecca's workgroup will create an interesting story.

fuzzy/performance

5 Between the hours of 7.00 p.m. and 7.00 a.m. Charles will remain in his own bed.

fuzzy/performance

6 Susie will sit on her Mum's lap and listen to a *Mister Man* story with interest.

fuzzy/performance

7 Sam's Dad needs to give him infinite supplies of love and compassion.

fuzzy/performance

8 Jean's teacher needs to give her lots and lots of individual attention.

fuzzy/performance

9 Jim will stop and wait at the edge of the kerb when his mother says "James, wait, please!"

fuzzy/performance

10 Jill will record on a chart whether or not she feels dizzy when she wakes up each morning.

fuzzy/performance

Hunt the fuzzy . . . Answers

1 A performance: Both Dad and Mum would say they were highly relieved to see Wayne was no longer playing dangerously.

2 A fuzzy: That word 'appreciate' has no precise definition.

3 A fuzzy: Not only that, it is not particularly good English!

4 A fuzzy: 'Stimulated' is not clear unless accompanied by a statement of 'how' also 'interest' is entirely dependent on subjective appraisal.

5 A performance: If Dad was awake he would be able to see Charlie happily lying in his own bed.

6 A fuzzy: We smell trouble when 'listening' and 'interest' are left to subjective assessment . . . can you get inside Susie's head to find out what is happening?

7 A fuzzy: How much is infinite – the blades of grass on a rugby pitch or the stars in the Milky Way – I don't know – do you? Love and compassion are as open to varying interpretation as there are writers and people.

8	A fuzzy:	'Lots and lots' may be even vaguer than 'infinite' and what is 'attention'?
9	A performance:	It couldn't be clearer, could it?
10	A performance:	It doesn't matter whether or not Jill is feeling dizzy, what matters is Dad can see her recording whatever she thinks she feels on her own chart.

Hunt the fuzzy

Postscript
Well, how did you do then? Let's see how many you got correct—

Correct Comments

10	Amazing! We may want to take lessons from you!
9 8	Well done! Pat yourself on the head and repeat several times the phrase "I did it"!
7	Not bad! Repeat the fuzzies test to see if you can get them all right second time around!
6 5 4	Try re-reading Chapter 2 and repeating the Test.
3 2 1	Try *reading* Chapter 2 before taking the Test next time.
0	Apply immediately for a senior post in Fuzzies Unlimited (or maybe we ought to rewrite the chapter!).

3

Where to begin

How to decide which problem to tackle first!

When someone says: "I just don't know what to do anymore, hitting her doesn't help", or "She's impossible, she never does anything I ask and she is always being rude", or "This school cannot contain him any longer. We've bent over backwards, but I can't ask the staff to go on taking his disgraceful behaviour", then a child's behaviour has reached a pretty unacceptable level. Statements like these tend to obscure problems.

Adults expect to be able to control children. When children are difficult many parents say they believe it is their fault. They feel they are failures. No one finds failure easy. We all react differently when in a tight spot with a difficult child.

In our clinic we have a two-way mirror. Sometimes we leave parents with their children playing in the playroom and retire to the other side of the glass to watch what happens. Often we see families playing happily but sometimes it goes wrong. The child will not do as he is told. We watch as the parents become more frenzied. Sometimes we see a child shaken, or hit while the mother says through gritted teeth, "You wait till I get you home!" Many parents point to a flaw in their child's character as the cause of the bad behaviour we observed. Others claim he always behaves like that because he takes after his Dad or a brother or some other relative recognised as the family's black sheep.

In our careful objective way we note all the antecedents and consequences of behaviours and can demonstrate sometimes that the behaviour was a result of things the parents did rather than the child being provocative.

By the time a psychologist becomes involved parents have often developed entrenched ideas about why their child behaves the way he does. In most instances when someone's behaviour has become a problem, people develop set views about the person. Very many claim the person will never change. Very many state categorically the child is evil and "has a devil in him". One parent may see the problem as "all his mother's fault; she's too soft with him!" Another may accuse her husband of causing the problem.

Although the way people say they see a problem is important and relevant to their perceptions it does not help change behaviour.

Thus to begin changing the child's behaviour we use a strategy which makes it possible for people to concentrate on specific problems – without clouding the issue by referring to past failed attempts, the alleged character deficiencies of the child, or the numerous events which have caused the child to be punished. This is simply to produce a P.P.L., or *Priority Problem List*.[3]

It is called a P.P.L. because the aim of the exercise is to decide which of all the behaviours the child exhibits the parents most want to change – *the priority problem.*

Constructing a P.P.L. makes it easier to take decisions about which problem should be tackled first. For the moment, we set aside our ABC of behaviour.

The Priority Problem List
There are four elements to a P.P.L.:
a positive comments about good behaviours (behaviour assets)
b statements describing the behaviour deficits and excesses which are problems
c an agreed priority problem
d the desired outcome of successfully treating the priority problem.

Who do you include?
The best people to complete this list are those who think that the child has a problem. Usually this will be the child's parents and teachers and another neutral person. A neutral person is needed, because as soon as

[3] Part of this method of dealing with problems was suggested by Thomas, E. J. and Walter, F. L. (1973) 'Guidelines for behavioural practice in the open community agency: procedures and evaluation' in *Journal of Behavioural Research and Therapy* Vol. 2, pages 193–205.

people start discussing such things they may get angry or tearful.

The neutral person is there not to act as judge and jury. She or he acts as a scribe and also helps the group to concentrate on the task of completing the P.P.L.

The other possible member of the group is the person whose behaviour is a problem. There are several instances where P.P.L.s have been written out with the person present.

This is not necessarily an unpleasant experience. Usually when a person knows his behaviour is causing others irritation, he predicts people are talking about him adversely. If he is included in the P.P.L. group he hears firstly the things people like about him, secondly a dispassionate discussion of his problems and finally is able to agree which of his behaviours will be changed first.

In cases where the person under discussion is very young or mentally handicapped then it is less likely he or she would be present.

It is wise, however, to collect together all adults who have direct contact with the person such as: playgroup leaders, nursery school or class teachers, and even brothers or sisters. It is important to realise that the group may be an uncommon collection of people because membership is determined by knowledge and contact with the person.

Therefore all those people who have sufficient contact with the child need to be brought together. In a junior school this could involve the class teacher, headteacher, parents, a dinner lady, a non-teaching assistant, and the caretaker. Since the group is on a fact-finding mission, anyone who has good information to submit should be invited to attend.

In entering information on a P.P.L. it is useful to know whether the child always reacts in the same way. It may be discovered that he will act in a certain way in response to his class teacher, and differently to a dinner lady. By having both present, the ABC of various incidents can be discussed. In the end, the whole group will be very clear about exactly what are the behaviours causing complaint.

When using a functional approach to problems there is no question of one person doing a right thing and another the wrong. The child's behaviour is seen as the result of a whole range of experiences and change being the responsibility not of one person but of the group.

Later, when all the problems have been identified, and the priority problem discussed in detail, the group will begin to devise strategies. At that stage it is important all the people who have daily contact with

the child know exactly what they should do when the priority problem arises.

In later chapters we will explain why *consistency* of handling is essential to create change. That is why, although it may be unusual for the school caretaker to sit down with the headteacher to discuss a child's behaviour, in some situations it is sensible as his information could provide solutions to problems. The caretaker's handling of the child when he catches him smoking in the cycle shed could have a profound effect on the child's behaviour. Therefore it is better that he and any other member of staff knows what has been agreed and understands what to do when the priority problem occurs.

P.P.L. – *The first step: positive comments*

The first thing to do is to think about positive features. What are all the desirable things the person does? All these good points are written down.

In reality, people always have difficulty in remembering the person's good points. It is not surprising, since the whole point of the meeting is that the person's behaviour has assumed proportions which force people to want to make him change. These are the behaviours which naturally crowd into the forefront of the discussion. But the good points are necessary because they may be important later when tackling problem behaviours.

Why do we want to know the good points? Often people plan to substitute good behaviour for problems when devising strategies. It is useful, therefore, to begin the session by highlighting positives. Quite apart from anything else, we have learnt to begin with a concentration on positive aspects which makes it fairly difficult for the session to degenerate into a non-productive 'bitching' session.

Under the heading *Positive comments: behaviour assets*, list at least three positive statements about the person, "He takes good care of his pet dog", "He helps with the washing up", "He says sorry after doing something wrong", "He isn't rude outside the house".

Note the comments should be written as performances. It truly is difficult sometimes to find any positive behaviours, so the odd fuzzy may creep in, "He seems to want to be trusted" is a monumental fuzzy. It is hard to know what this means, but after discussion, a performance statement might emerge. Some fuzzies pop up because peoples' impression of positives are vague as there are so few of them. The

Working through a P.P.L.

professional or friend helping with the list may end up nudging people into more positive comments by asking questions which clarify fuzzy statements about good behaviour.

P.P.L. – The second step: problems
The second step; statements about behaviour deficits and excesses which are a problem.

It is predictable people will find it easy to remember the problems. Each behaviour should be written as a performance! People are tempted to make global comments like, "He's disruptive and aggressive towards the rest of the group", or "He's into everything so he can't be left alone". When this happens, the scribe and others in the group should ask questions like, "What would I see him doing when he is being disruptive?" or "What exactly happens when he is being aggressive?"

This part of the P.P.L. describes the things people most want to change, therefore such statements should highlight performances precisely and be clear to everyone.

Comments in the problems section might say something like "Stuart is late for meals" or "John will not stay in bed at night", which are behaviours causing inconvenience in the smooth running of a household. The section might also describe the way the child behaves towards others in the family, "Henry hits his sister", or "Julie tries to push Joseph off my lap when I am reading to him", or "He hides in the cloakroom whenever my mother comes to the house". The list might also contain information about undesirable personal habits, "Maria chews her nails. She has bitten down to the quick on both hands", or "John pinches anyone who comes near him", or even "Fred bangs his head all the time on the floor or wall".

Sometimes it is difficult for the scribe to remain neutral. There is a temptation to leap in and tell everyone where they are going wrong. There may even seem to him to be obvious solutions which are difficult to keep quiet about.

There are wide variations between families in their rule systems. One family may allow their children to remain up until late. In another, a fifteen-year-old may be expected to be in bed by nine on school days. It does not matter if the scribe thinks that one family is too lax and the other too strict. It is irrelevant to the families' decision making process. What is relevant is that the scribe lists the behaviours in neat performance terms, checks back where necessary, and keeps the group on task so that the decision making process is made as easy as possible.

P.P.L. – The third step: selecting a priority problem
As the list grows some behaviours begin to stick out as more important than others, some begin to pale into insignificance. Sometimes links between positives and problems begin to emerge. Eventually when no one can think of another good or bad behaviour the group begins to discuss the child's most intolerable behaviour; the agreed priority problem.

There are more pitfalls waiting to trap the over-eager scribe at this point. It is easy for a scribe, especially if a professional, to slip into the trap of deciding *for* the parents which is the problem behaviour. Even next door neighbours can trip up in the same way. How often have you discussed a minor problem with a close friend and ended the chat being given advice on how to change your entire life style to alter something which for *you* was not a burning issue at all?

An important rule to remember is parents and teachers know about *their* lives, *their* homes, *their* classrooms. They can determine which problem on a problem list is the most important, which behavioural deficit or excess causes greatest distress or most handicaps the child. The problem list makes it possible for them to list problems and identify a priority. People almost invariably need help to arrive at this point and this is a useful service which any professional psychologist or social worker should be well equipped to offer.

Groups producing problem lists can generally agree fairly easily which is the problem behaviour they would most like to change. To anyone from outside the family or group their choice may not seem obvious. Their decision is based on a day-to-day involvement with the person and they know only too well which is the worst deficit or excess in their own particular setting.

If a problem list is made with parents, teachers and maybe even the dinner staff present it is possible the group will have difficulty selecting a priority. Each group of people may be finding a different problem the worst to handle. As an example this was a problem list constructed within school with parents, teachers, the dinner supervisors, the head-teacher and a psychologist present.

Jack's P.P.L.

A *Positive comments*
1 He has an endless supply of Irish jokes to tell.
2 He is very kind to small animals and cleans out and feeds the classroom gerbils each day.

3 His handwriting is neat.
4 Jack does his number work well, he gets his sums right every day.

B *Problems*
a Swearing: he uses four letter words.
b Pinching: he pinches adults or children (and it hurts).
c When told 'no' *in any situation*, he kicks, screams, punches and swears. He can maintain a temper tantrum for up to ten minutes.
d Destroying books: he chews the corners and sometimes whole pages.
e Wandering away: if left unattended near an open door, he slips out into the open street.
f Scribbling on walls: this is restricted to the cloakrooms and certain dark areas of the school where parents, staff and other adults rarely penetrate.

All these behaviours occurred both in school and at home. When discussing which problem was the priority the parents instantly picked the tantrum behaviour, the teachers picked swearing and the dinner supervisors were most concerned about scribbling.

Their choices related directly to their experiences at home, in class and during playtime. The parents were remembering horrific scenes at the checkouts of supermarkets, their other children in tears after one of Jack's tantrums at home, and the exasperation and tiredness they felt after a bad day. The teachers were able to share out Jack's tantrums by putting him in a different class, isolating him or sending him away with a non-teaching ancillary. It was the swearing which caused them inconvenience, with a stream of parents coming to school and complaining that their children who had never before uttered such words were now using the many colourful swear words Jack had in his vocabulary. The dinner supervisors did not have to experience many tantrums and the swearing caused them little concern. It was the walls in the toilet covered with juvenile graffiti, the anger of the caretakers and the problems of keeping anything resembling pens, pencils, biro, crayon or even lipstick away from the boy which caused them greatest irritation.

After much discussion in which the professional did little but listen and ensure every group member had an opportunity to express their opinions, the group selected tantrum behaviour as the priority problem. The parents persuaded the school staff that if they could teach

Jack to accept 'no' then many of his other behaviours would be easier to bring under control.

P.P.L. – *The fourth step: the desired outcome*

The final, most important element of a P.P.L. is: *specifying the result of overcoming the problem behaviour.*

The end result of a P.P.L. is to state a desired outcome which is a description of what will be happening when a change has been made.

The statement of the Priority Problem and the result of overcoming the problem behaviour are often seen like two sides of the same coin. If the Priority Problem is seen as "He is involved in three or more fights in class each day", the expression of the desired outcome might be the opposite, i.e. "He has no fights in class". But although that may well be the desired outcome, living in the real world means that we recognise all human beings are fallible and some targets are just too hard to reach immediately. So the group might set out an intermediate target which can be reached more easily, e.g. "No more than three fights a week".

In Jack's case, the result of overcoming his problem was expressed as "Jack will be able to accept 'no' from any adult with whom he has regular contact, without having a temper tantrum or kicking, punching, screaming or swearing".

By the time the problem list is lying neatly on a sheet of paper, all those who took part in the discussion should be much clearer about the real problems, caused by the person under discussion. The group should know that whatever their 'memories' tell them and whatever 'attitudes' they have developed towards the person, he or she has good as well as bad points. Best of all they should have agreed a definite behavioural change they all want to see.

Paul's P.P.L.

The P.P.L. opposite was written by a mother. She used the P.P.L. framework. She had no trouble in identifying *her* Priority Problem, "Paul says 'won't' when asked to dress himself each morning".

Revision: Goggle box June

Although very helpful around the house, June aged eleven is a bit disorganised. Sometimes she helps her Mum prepare the evening meal, but often forgets to do essential things like putting salt in the potatoes or she lets the vegetables burn.

The trouble is that June is a TV addict. Both she and her father are

Paul's P.P.L.

POSITIVES

1. He talks to the baby and makes me laugh.
2. ~~He's very loving~~
   He sits on my knee and hugs me.
3. He always cleans his plate and never fusses at mealtimes.
4. Sometimes he plays in the garden with the boy next door for hours at a time.
5. He helps me when we go shopping.
6. He makes me laugh a lot.

PROBLEMS

1. ~~Fights with Jean~~. He pulls Jean's hair if when she won't share a toy or sometimes a game.
2. Sulks when I say No. (Usually at bedtime)
3. ~~Says won't always questioning instructions~~
   Says "won't" when asked to get dressed in the morning. ~~I have to dress him most of the time.~~
4. Sits too near the tele.
5. Turns on taps and leaves them on.

PRIORITY PROBLEM

3. Not dressing in the morning.

WHAT I WOULD LIKE TO SEE HAPPENING

Paul will get dressed on his own. Except for his shoes. (To put on underpants, socks, vest, tee shirt, trousers)

Nb. on weekdays only. Weekends don't matter so much.

crazy about old films and spend ages discussing these together. When a film is being shown on the TV everything else takes second place whether it is helping with the meal, tidying her bedroom or finishing off her homework.

Just recently, her form teacher told June, she had received several complaints from other teachers. These were about uncompleted or missing homework assignments. She warned her that she would have to mend her ways. June's classwork on the other hand was quite satisfactory and she was top of her class in Maths. However, something had to be done about these homework assignments . . .

June's mother wrote out a P.P.L. with positives and problems listed. Then she selected a priority problem and stated a desired outcome. On page 48 is the contract eventually worked out between June and her Dad – more on this subject in Chapter 5.

June's P.P.L.

POSITIVES

1. Helps around the house, e.g. preparing meals.
2. She and Dad share an interesting hobby.
3. Classwork satisfactory.
4. Top of class in Maths.

PROBLEMS

1. Forgets to put salt in potato pot.
2. Lets the vegetables burn.
3. Does not keep her room tidy.
4. Watches the T.V. instead of completing her homework.

PRIORITY PROBLEM

Watches T.V. instead of completing her homework.

DESIRED OUTCOME — What I would like to see happening.

June would complete her homework before nine o'clock each weeknight and would show it to her Dad.

A CONTRACT BETWEEN JUNE AND DAD

I undertake to complete my homework assignment each evening before settling down to watch television. I will also undertake to show my completed homework to Dad before the nine o'clock news in case any alterations need to be made to it.

Signed

June

If all homework assignments for one week have been completed as agreed. I will allow June to stay up on Friday night to watch the midnight movie with me. I also undertake not to talk about the film stars when the most exciting parts of the Midnight movie occur.

Signed

Dad.

4

Stepping stones

Planning a teaching programme

Sometimes the chosen target behaviour seems ambitious and even unattainable. Such a target would cause comments like, "I can't see him doing that in a hurry", or "It would take a miracle for her to manage that", or "I have been trying to do that for the last six months and nothing has happened".

You know the kind of situation. Someone in the family says "I'm going to give up smoking tomorrow", and is met with a universal cry of disbelief. Or in a women's magazine we see the sylph-like form of an eight-stone beauty and can hardly believe she achieved that target from a starting point of eighteen stone. What mother has not cried "Oh for the day when he is dry, will it ever come?" when up to her elbows in soapsuds and dirty nappies?

When target behaviours seem hopelessly ambitious there is no need to abandon hope and scrap the whole idea. There is an effective system to bring those targets into your grasp.

A good method for looking at targets which at first seem impossible is to call them *long-term targets* and to say they will be reached not after a week or after a month, but after several months or even years. A long-term target seems closer after filling in a series of steps or shorter term targets. Then a person can see how, by easy stages, each one simple in itself, the long-term target will become possible.

There is nothing new about breaking down big targets into a number of small ones. Consider a beginners' class in swimming; what horror and dismay there would be if the instructor lined the class up at the deep end of the swimming pool and said, "Okay, folks, dive in!" Wise instructors make their clients happy in a first swimming lesson. They help them to flop around in the shallow end of the pool wearing armbands, or maybe kicking their legs up and down while holding on safely to the edge of the pool.

How many clients would a driving instructor have if on the first lesson he invited his student to drive round Hyde Park Corner while he read a newspaper?

Those targets, diving into the deep end of the swimming pool or driving in busy traffic, are common teenage dreams which most achieve with time and practice. Trying to get there in the first five minutes of instruction would be a case of 'too much, too soon', for almost everyone. Yet anyone can reach those goals if they are guided safely through the easy stages like hanging on to the side of the pool, or being taught to start the car, to change gear without help and to drive a mile along a quiet, straight back street. In either case in each lesson the student knows if he reaches the target set. Through a series of lessons in which many small achievements will be chalked up, the pupil will reach those ultimate long-term targets of swimming three lengths of the pool using butterfly stroke, or driving a car in the rush hour unaccompanied.

The process used to break down a long-term target behaviour into a number of smaller easy steps or stages is called *task analysis.*

Other examples of task analyses crop up everywhere. When new pieces of equipment are purchased, the wrappings usually contain step-by-step instructions on how to assemble, operate or repair. These are informal examples of a task analysis. Similarly all good do-it-yourself books contain well prepared analyses of the various tasks people may want to undertake in their home unaided by an 'expert'.

Consider the problem posed by repairing a burnt out or damaged fuse in a plug, difficult for the naïve but the instructions make it simple indeed:

1 Have ready small screwdriver and replacement fuse.
2 Remove plug from socket.
3 Slacken off large screw until plug comes apart.
4 Gently prise worn fuse out.
5 Throw old fuse in bin.
6 Carefully replace new fuse in receiving brackets.
7 Match up two pieces of plug and tighten large screw until both pieces fit snugly together.
8 Replace plug in socket and check that electrical appliance works.

This example illustrates that there are four major components of a task analysis. These are:

A clear statement of what the task consists.
The tools or materials required to complete the task.
The starting point.
A proceed line in a series of easy steps.

When analysing the breaking down of a long-term target into smaller steps these four components must be included.

Most children learn to dress themselves by a series of steps as they achieve various skill levels. Occasionally a child has difficulty. What are the steps most children proceed through as they learn to choose appropriate clothes and dress themselves? See if you can add anything to this list.

1 Pulls off socks.
2 Pushes arms through sleeves, legs through pants.
3 Takes off shoes when unfastened.
4 Takes off coat when unfastened.
5 Unzips large zip fastener.
6 Puts on shoes.
7 Takes off clothes when these have been unfastened.
8 Unfastens press-studs.
9 Puts on socks.
10 Puts on coat, sweater, shirt, etc. (not always the correct way round).
11 Finds front of clothing.
12 Dresses self with help on pullovers, shirts and all fasteners.
13 Snaps together press-studs.
14 Unbuttons large buttons.
15 Buttons large buttons.
16 Puts on overcoat without help.
17 Unbuttons small buttons.
18 Buttons small buttons.
19 Puts zipper foot into catch and does up zipper.
20 Dresses self completely, except ties and shoe laces.
21 Ties shoe laces.
22 Dresses without help.
23 Hangs up clothes after dressing.
24 Chooses correct clothes for (a) location (b) occasion and (c) weather conditions.

To acquire many of these skills, most children will only require lots of encouragement, others may need a little help from their parents or brothers and sisters, and for a small number of skills, e.g. buttons, zips, shoe laces and so on, they will have to be taught very carefully how to do these.

Sometimes, however, some children may find great difficulty in moving from one stage to another. In fact, sometimes the step from one skill to the next is just too big. In such circumstances it would be necessary to carry out a task analysis.

If, for example, parents or teachers were wanting to help a child to put on her shoes without help then this would be our *long-term target*. To proceed to that point it would be necessary to find out exactly what skills the child has already acquired. In this case, it might well be that the child could take off her shoes when her mother had unfastened them. This is the *present* skill level. Now it is necessary to choose one easy new skill which this little girl could attain very quickly. This might be locating left and right shoes correctly and placing the shoes together in front of her. This would then be our *easy first step*. A possible *sequence of steps* to fill the gap between our long-term target and easy first step could be:

1 Puts shoes on correct feet (mother does up buckle).
2 Puts shoes on correct feet, does up buckle (mother tucks in loose end).
3 Puts shoes on correct feet, does up buckle and tucks in loose end.

Again, this simple task analysis has got all the necessary elements. These are:

A long-term target: Sharon will put on her shoes without help.
A statement of what the child can do now: Sharon can take off her shoes when these have been unfastened.
An easy first step: Sharon will locate left and right shoes correctly and place shoes together in front of her.
A sequence of steps showing how to proceed: Sharon will put her shoes on correctly, while mother does up buckle: Sharon will put her shoes on correctly, fasten buckle and mother will tuck in loose end.

Task analysis guidelines
To complete a task analysis take a large blank sheet of white paper and write down the following:

1 The long-term teaching target – psychologists sometimes call such a target the 'target behaviour' or the 'behavioural objective'.
2 What the person can do at the moment. This is a precise performance description (no fuzzies!) of the person's skill level at present.
3 *One* target the person should reach in a relatively short time, e.g. a week (or a month at the maximum).
4 A sequence of steps to fill the gap between the first target outlined in 3 and the long-term target outlined in 1.

Task analysis is not always easy, but in almost any situation where learning a task appears difficult compiling one usually helps the teacher plan a better teaching programme. The following task analysis demonstrates the method used once more:

The messy dustbin man

Housewives complain regularly about that weekly visitor: the dustbin man. Obviously some dustbin men do everything housewives want them to do, but sometimes these very essential people cause women to grumble, gripe and even mutter nasty rude things under their breath about dustbin men in general, and one or two in particular. In this case the housewife was irritated every Thursday by having to retrieve her dustbin lid from the road and picking up all the bits and pieces spilt between her gate and the dustcart. She sat down and wrote the following task analysis:

1 *Long-term target*	The dustbin man ('B-Man') will collect the bin from outside the kitchen door, which is twenty feet inside the garden gate. He will empty the dustbin without spilling more than three items, and replace the lid correctly on the empty dustbin.
2 *Present point which B-Man has reached*	The B-Man will empty the dustbin if it is outside the front gate. He spills an average of nine items and either jams the lid inside the dustbin or throws it on an average seven feet down the street.
3 *Next possible target which the B-Man should reach in a month. (Step One)*	The B-Man will leave the bin lid within six inches of the empty dustbin at the front gate.

4 *Possible sequence of steps to attain long-term goal already specified*

Step Two. The B-Man will replace the lid squarely on the empty bin outside the front gate.

Step Three. The B-Man will spill no more than eight items and put the lid squarely on the empty bin outside the front gate.

Step Four. The B-Man will not spill more than five items and put the lid squarely on the empty bin, outside the gate.

Step Five. The B-Man will spill no more than three items and put the lid squarely on the empty bin outside the front gate.

Step Six. The B-Man will go through the front gate and collect the bin from just inside the gate about seventeen inches up the path. He will not spill more than three items. He will replace the lid correctly on the empty bin *inside* the front gate.

Step Seven. The B-Man will walk six feet up the path, empty the dustbin spilling no more than three items. He will replace the lid correctly on the empty bin and leave it inside the gate.

Step Eight. The B-Man will walk up to the front of the house, empty the dustbin (spilling only three items). He will replace the lid correctly on the empty bin and leave it where he found it.

Step Nine. The B-Man will walk up past the side of the house to the kitchen door and pick up the bin. He will empty the bin, only spilling three items, and replace the lid correctly on the empty bin.

He will leave it by the kitchen door and collect his Christmas gratuity from the grateful house-wife.

This housewife was not writing down *how* these steps would be reached, but was using the task analysis technique to break down what she perceived as a highly ambitious target into a number of smaller and readily attainable steps. In fact this particular housewife solved the problem by accident. On a wet and windy Thursday, having overslept, she staggered down the pathway carrying the over-full bin wearing little more than a silk dressing gown and a smile. The gallant, chival-rous instincts of the dustbin men must have been aroused since from then on they did what she desired!

Unknowingly, what the housewife had done was to change the background within which the bin-emptying behaviour occurred. More than that, the dustbin man may have thought that the consequences might also one day change.

Just as dustbin men can irritate housewives, reports and letters in our local press indicate that dustbin men become annoyed by the behaviour of some of their clients. A dustbin man might write a task analysis for an ambitious target which would make his working life more pleasant.

His targets could be to teach the housewife to do helpful things, like wrapping broken glass in newspaper and putting rubbish in containers that do not rot in the bin, and talking to the dustbin man rather than complaining directly to the Council. He might find the housewife at the *present point* of behaviour:

Present point which H-wife has reached

H-Wife puts out broken glass beside dustbin in thin plastic bags. She puts rubbish into old card-board boxes. She does not tie a knot in the dustbin bags, so the garbage often falls out over the dustbin man as he empties it into the dustcart. She phones the Council about once a month to complain about his service.

Next possible target which the housewife could reach in one month. H-Wife will wrap broken glass in a newspaper before putting it into the plastic bag or put a label on the bag: 'broken glass'.

Why don't you pretend to be the dustbin man and write out the steps of this task analysis to achieve his long-term target?

Step One

Step Two

Step Three

Step Four

Step Five

Step Six

Different routes to success
Other housewives or dustbin men might have chosen different steps to reach the desired target behaviours. This is not only perfectly reasonable but absolutely inevitable. There are many paths to success in any enterprise. What matters is that the steps will enable the person to reach his goal eventually.

In writing task analyses and working out the steps between short- and long-term goals, the difficulty is placing the steps in a logical sequence. Each step should be made easier by the ones before it. It may be that the steps in the first draft of an analysis are too big and the gaps may need to be filled with smaller steps. Conversely sometimes people skip several steps at a time improving their performance in the desired direction swiftly and dramatically. When this happens open the champagne and celebrate because the first steps were obviously spot on target.

People's background, their experiences and inventiveness will determine the steps they choose when writing a task analysis. There is no right way in the sense of an *only* way to reach any given point.

Often parents of young children find it difficult to leave them playing a game quietly together. Two sets of parents were asked to work out a task analysis. The target behaviour was that Sally aged six would play quietly with her young sister Mary (aged two and a half) for at least half an hour.

The parents were told that at the present time Mary played a game of skittles on her own provided her mother was present to help.

The first set of parents broke the problem down into several steps which started with the mother fully involved and helping Mary right through the game. The mother would then withdraw. She would sit on a chair watching, when necessary telling Mary what to do, and praising them when they did well. Then she would leave the room for long enough for her two daughters each to have a turn. Gradually she lengthened the time she left the children alone until she was away for the full half hour.

The other parents chose to take part fully and gradually increase the number of turns each child took until the game was lasting for ten minutes. The length of time the children played together, with both parents present and helping was increased. The parents gradually gave less help but remained present to praise and encourage. Eventually Sally and Mary played together for the desired half hour period in the same manner as the other parents suggested.

Both approaches would have reached the target behaviour. One shows how activities can be learned by *reducing the assistance* given, while the other approach concentrates on *increasing the difficulty* of the task.

The secret of successfully working out task analyses is two-fold. The first part is an analysis of the task. The second is devising the simplest most logical sequence by which to teach those subskills. It sounds easy enough, but like most things it requires practice. Try working an analysis for the following long-term target:

Long-term goal	Jean will tidy away her toys into the toy cupboard when asked.
Present status	Jean will put six to eight toys in a box *only* when handed them by her mother.
Next possible target which Jean can reach in one week.	*Step One*
	Step Two
	Step Three
	Step Four

There are several ways of reaching this target. One person might increase the number of toys which Jean puts into the box. Another might teach Jean to pick up an increasing number of toys scattered around the room and at a later stage place them in the toy box. Some people might have wanted to teach Jean the separate ascending scales of picking up toys when asked, putting them in the toy box, and moving the toy box to the cupboard door, placing it in the cupboard, and finally shutting the cupboard door.

In fact, if an analysis is completed logically, sometimes the writer uncovers a quick route to the long-term target. The father who faced the scattered toy problem found such a short cut. When he looked at his completed task analysis, it was obvious that the picking up of the toys was not only hard work but tedious. To overcome these aspects, he found a one-step solution.

The toy box was painted bright red. Bright yellow wheels and a handle were fitted. He painted "Toy Transporter" along the sides. Then he taught his untidy daughter to circuit the living room picking up loose toys in her super new truck.

5

Teaching new behaviour

How people learn new skills and how to make learning easy

Who has not said, "Hey, look at that, I did it!" It may have been something which to other people was fairly simple like tying a shoe lace or, something as difficult as passing a driving test.

According to history Archimedes was so delighted when he understood the principles of volume that he leapt out of the bath and ran naked, jumping for joy, through the streets of Athens calling out "Eureka, Eureka!"

History books reveal the laws of gravity dropped into Newton's lap from an overladen tree but do not tell us how he expressed his reactions! Both of them had made unique discoveries without any teacher around to make life easy.

Who teaches?
For the rest of us, successful acquisition of new knowledge is usually made possible by someone who teaches. That someone may or may not be a 'teacher' in the normal sense. Everybody is at some time a teacher whether they realise it or not. Children do not just start crawling, walking, running, hopping or jumping. Adults teach them!

On rare occasions children have been discovered in remote deserts living with groups of gazelles. These children instead of learning to walk and run as we do and speak, have been observed to move like their gazelle foster parents. Such children apparently run with long loping strides at speeds far faster than modern man is able, and convey messages by ear twitching, nose moving, or stamping on the ground. They have been seen to eat a vegetable diet of grass and leaves. These children who possibly became detached as small babies from wandering bands of nomads who live in the desert, have learned from their gazelle foster families the skills for survival as part of an animal group. Had they grown up with their natural parents they would have learned to behave like anyone else in their tribe or society.

Parental teaching is informal. It would be an unusual event for a parent to say at breakfast, "Today, I will teach my child to walk." It would be equally unusual for a parent to plan a situation to teach a child to wash his face, clean his teeth or make a pot of tea. Gradually, parents teach these and many other skills as occasions naturally occur, making teaching or learning easy.

The skills parents teach their children are so obvious and fundamental that it is not necessary for them to analyse the situation beforehand and identify which skills to teach. Or at least that is true until a child with problems happens along. Once parents are faced with a child with special needs, whether those result from physical and mental handicaps or relate to a child with problem behaviours, informal teaching has to give way to a more planned approach.

But doing things naturally is different from doing them formally. Sometimes people expect it will be difficult to teach formally. Parenthood is perhaps one of the most important roles human beings adopt and yet few are taught except by example how to cope. Planned teaching is a new skill for most parents and as such can be initially daunting.

In fact teaching is not difficult if the right components are fitted into a programmed framework. If a child learns to name the members of his family, make requests or talk to an adult, to play on his own or play with another, then he learned these things because certain features were present in the teaching. He would have had opportunities to see the behaviour, to practise behaving in a way which pleased others. These necessary elements would have been fitted into the framework, by those who taught him, quite without deliberate planning.

The teaching formula
When someone tries to teach something new, the way to make the exercise foolproof and speedily successful is to make sure the teaching programme includes several fundamental elements. These essential features fall into three sections:

1 Preparation ⎤
2 Planning ⎬   the three 'Ps' of successful teaching
3 Performing ⎦

Preparation

The foundation of teaching is preparation. We described the elements of this foundation in Chapters 2, 3 and 4 when we discussed the identification and definition of behaviour and the necessity of stating a desired final outcome for any teaching programme. Sometimes it seems obvious to everyone what changes are required. Someone might say, "Boy, has he got a temper" or "None of our family has been able to count". But even if we know roughly where the problem lies, the teacher must know exactly what is the skill he intends to teach. Thus the problem behaviour needs to be identified in performance terms without a 'fuzzy' in sight. E.g. John will not accept 'no' from his mother without throwing a tantrum, or, Fiona cannot add more than four items correctly.

When any behaviour is described this clearly it is a simple matter to write down the desired outcome. E.g. John will accept 'no' from his mother without argument four out of five occasions, or, Fiona will be able to count ten objects correctly.

When there seems to be a large number of problems causing concern, making a problem list is the best way to select a priority problem.

The last vital bit of the jigsaw needed in the preparation phase is using a task analysis to plan a teaching programme. This will outline the little steps which bridge the gaps between present skill level and desired target behaviours.

The most important rule in teaching is "Never put a pupil in a position where failure is almost inevitable." Once someone has been asked to do something which is way beyond their capabilities, even though it is simple for the person teaching, the experience is unpleasant and the pupil is often unwilling to try other new things with that person again. The consequences for the teacher are not good either. The pupil's failure can produce a whole range of teacher responses like anger, or worse: the conviction the child will never succeed. The minutes or even hours spent in logically analysing the component sub-skills of any activity are *never ever* wasted. Even simple tasks which we do every day are quite complicated when broken down into individual skill components.

Once a nurse in a centre for the adult mentally handicapped wanted to teach a patient how to prepare his own breakfast as part of a self-help programme. She used a task analysis and discovered there were no less than fourteen different steps involved in what had seemed a remarkably simple exercise: preparing a grapefruit and eating it! It's true. You try it!

Happily she successfully taught the patient this and many other skills and eventually he moved out into a self-catering hostel in the town.

Revision: Preparation

Preparing to teach means:
1 Listing the behaviours which need to be learned.
2 Selecting a priority.
3 Writing down the desired outcome.
4 If necessary, planning a step-by-step teaching programme by task analysis.
5 Clearly stating an initial teaching target.

Planning

Once the foundation of the framework; good 'preparation' has been laid, the next bit of work is planning the functional requirements for teaching. These consist of the *place* where the teaching will occur, the *materials* needed for the pupil to carry out the activity, the *method* by which the skill is going to be taught and how progress will be *recorded*.

The choice of a *place* for teaching is not obvious.

A teacher in a school can choose several places within one classroom for teaching. The choice could cover: standing by the blackboard and talking, having the pupil by her desk, standing over the pupil at his desk, working at a specific bench or table, side by side, or, even, sitting together on the floor. At home, teaching could happen in any room or area of the house or garden – or even in the garage! Making this choice will be influenced by the nature of the skill being taught and by the pupil's physical size and ability.

The teaching session is more likely to succeed if carried out in a prearranged place where the necessary materials have been assembled. There is nothing more off-putting for a pupil, than to wait around doing nothing while someone organises bits and pieces and then, to be asked to do something in a place or position which makes it difficult. For instance, it may be far easier for a child to colour in while sitting on the floor or at a low table, than sitting on adult chairs at the kitchen table. It is better to have a child who is distractable on his or her own rather than in a crowded room. It is obviously easier for the novice rider to be taken into a small enclosed area for the first lesson than let loose in a large field. Toiletting and feeding skills are more easily taught in the rooms where these activities usually occur than in other parts of the house.

When the place has been decided *all* the *materials* should be assembled. The teacher should be able to produce the materials in the correct sequence at the optimum moment in the teaching session. Some of the success of the teaching rests in the pupil's perception of the competence of the teacher whether it is his mother, aunt, school teacher, local garage mechanic or best friend. Fumbling around looking for a bit of kit, unwrapping a large parcel to remove one small item, or having to leave the room to fetch a forgotten essential book makes a teaching session sloppy, introduces moments of 'do nothing' time for the pupil, in which he can forget that which went before or just lose interest in the session.

Before introducing the pupil to the situation and the materials, the teacher should have a written or clearly thought out plan of *how to teach the skill*. This is not just the task analysis. This plan covers *how the skill will be demonstrated, how the pupil will be asked to complete the tasks, how mistakes will be corrected, successes celebrated and progress recorded.* Recording may involve the use of a chart or some other system.

This may seem like a lot of work, a lot of time devoted to pre-organisational detail. In practice, it is not and it is better to spend time completing this framework so that the eyeball to eyeball confrontation of a teaching session is easy for both teacher and pupil, than rushing into teaching and ending up spending hours which culminate in partial success or worse – failure.

But all this careful planning can be seriously undermined if thought is not given to the way in which the teaching session could progress.

Two things can happen for the pupil: he can be successful or he can fail. He may not be sure the first time he tries something precisely what he is expected to do, or whether he has reached the teacher's desired level of success. The teacher may rightly believe that his initial demonstration was perfect and comprehensible by his pupil. His pupil, however, may experience uncertainty while he tries to do as his teacher directed in many, though certainly not all, instances. It is necessary for the teacher to think through his directions and explanations and decide at which points in the pupil's performance he is going to encourage his pupil, by making positive statements concerning his success. These

'Do nothing' time encourages pupils to do something else

intimations of success, during and after the pupil has completed the activity, should occur in a manner which makes the pupil want to carry out the activity again.

Comments like, "Weren't you watching?", "You put that there, not here!" or "Well, you did that wrong, in fact you didn't get anything right", are less likely to make the pupil try again willingly than remarks like, "You did well remembering this bit, but that bit went here not there" or "That was a good try, let's do it again together and then you see if you can get it right". The wisest teacher, however, does not get into these difficulties at all. Preventing failure depends on anticipating which bits of the activity are going to present particular problems and teaching those elements in extremely small steps or, creating a correction procedure. Usually a correction procedure involves the pupil completing the task with as much help as necessary.

It is helpful to the pupil and teacher if successes and difficulties are *recorded* in some way. Suppose half an hour is spent trying to master the sounds of three different letters. By the end of the period the pupil will be more eager to try again if the teacher is able to say, "Well, you tried to read this letter twelve times and were right on eight" or "Look how many times you were right, you've learned that really well!" Recording has added benefits. A teacher has a constant check on what she has tried to teach, what the child has apparently learned and what still has to be practised.

Recording can operate at the simple level of ticking on a sheet of paper when the child is successful. There are more sophisticated methods which are also more fun and some of those are described in the next section.

Revision: Planning
1 Selecting the *place* where teaching will occur.
2 Assembling the necessary teaching *materials*.
3 Deciding the *directions, explanations and demonstrations* required for the teaching session.
4 Deciding how to celebrate success or correct failure.
5 Designing a method to *record progress*.

Performing
In approaching the teaching task through preparation and planning as outlined, we are once more demonstrating the importance of the ABC of behaviour.

When teaching, the aim is to control all the important antecedent, background and consequent events. If the correct balance between these three is achieved the teaching will be successful.

The directions to the child in words and actions of what he is required to do form the *antecedent* events. Therefore they must be clear, unambiguous and precisely relevant to the task.

The place where the teaching will occur and all the materials to be used form the *background* to the behaviour. Hence by assembling the right bits and pieces and choosing an appropriate position or area for instruction the teacher is achieving control over the second important element of behaviour – background.

Finally, by deciding how successes will be celebrated and encouraged, failures corrected, and results recorded, the teacher also brings *consequent* events under control.

The actual performance of teaching a task should follow this sequence:

1 *Direct* the pupil using explanations and actions if necessary.
2 *Lead* the pupil through the task.
3 *Invite* the pupil to complete the task unaided.
4 *Celebrate* success or *correct* inaccurate performance.
5 *Practise* until the task has been learned.
6 *Record* the results of the teaching session.
N.B. Step 2 may not always be necessary.

One of the neatest examples of this framework in use was developed by members of a team working in Wisconsin, U.S.A. They pioneered a home teaching scheme for families with a handicapped child. The system was called the Portage Project and was introduced to the U.K. in 1976.

The Portage Project is now well established in Hampshire where we work as well as other parts of England. The Wessex Health Care Evaluation Research Team in Winchester, Hampshire, were the first to adopt the system. They have been using the framework to teach new skills not only to handicapped pre-school children but also to adults including old people in residential homes. Using the framework, the Wessex team have demonstrated that 90 per cent of all skills they have taught have been successfully attained.[4]

[4]Cameron, R. J. (1979) 'A lot can happen at home too', *Journal of Remedial Education* November.

The Wessex team use a specially designed sheet called an Activity Chart, as a primary teaching aid. The illustration on page 70 shows the elements of an Activity Chart. Many of the points discussed under preparation and planning are included in an Activity Chart. The chart simplifies the preparation and planning stages by acting as an *aide-mémoire.*

In the Portage Project, home teachers make weekly visits to parents of a handicapped child. The home teacher is with the parents for roughly an hour and a half. The performance of the child during the previous week is checked. The mother shows what has been learned and a new target behaviour is agreed for the coming week. This target would probably be a small step on the way to a major target. The chart is completed in the following fashion.

Teaching target
The parent and the teacher agree on a target behaviour which they want the child to learn in the next week.

This is written down in performance terms (NO FUZZIES). E.g. Robert will place six red and six yellow beads on six red and six yellow circles drawn on a card.

Number of practices
The parent and teacher decide the number of times the task will be practised daily. This number is entered on the chart. The teaching would probably happen with the mother doing some practices in the morning and maybe more in the afternoon or evening until she had completed the agreed number. It would be unusual for the mother to have one lengthy teaching session to complete the day's assignment. On Portage, little and often is better than an overdose.

Success rate
The criterion is set for success. It might be agreed that the child would be able to perform the target behaviour with 75 per cent accuracy or maybe as high as 100 per cent by the end of the week. The criterion would be decided upon by considering how well the child was carrying out earlier steps of the task and predicting what he should be able to achieve after one week's teaching.

Recording
Recording the results of some or all of the practice trials gives an accurate statement of how the child is progressing to both parent and

ACTIVITY CHART

Child's name

Starting date

Teaching target

Write here the behaviour you want to see the child doing in one week's time.

How often to practise

Write here the number of times you want the child to carry out the activity each day.

Success rate

What level of success do you expect your child to reach after one weeks practice.

What to record

Write down the number of times you want to record the outcome of your teaching trials on the vertical line of the graph. Write the days of the week along the horizontal line beginning on the first day of teaching.

Teaching trials recorded each day

Days of the week

Materials

Mention each item or toy which you will use.

Place of work

Make it clear where you and the child will carry out the activity e.g. on the floor, table ....

Directions

Write down exactly what you will do and say to get your child to carry out the activity which you are teaching.

Success procedure

Write down what you will do to show your child that he or she has attained the target behaviour. This must be clearly different to your response when the child requires help to attain the target.

Correction procedure

What minimum aid you will provide if the child requires help to reach the target. This will be one of the following depending on the child – giving a verbal correction, modelling the correct behaviour or physically guiding the child through the activity.

How to record

This is usually done by recording a √ if the child attains the target or a ⊘ if you used one of the correction procedures.

home teacher. The number of trials the parent agrees to record is entered on the vertical axis on the outside of the chart. The days of the week are entered on the horizontal axis starting with the day of the week which is the first day of teaching. The first day of teaching is called the 'baseline' performance. The day on which the child should have achieved the skill is known as the 'post baseline' performance. The method of recording is also agreed. A tick, or check mark, is usually used by parents to show when the child performed correctly. Often a tick within a circle is chosen to represent the child performing correctly, but with help. The agreed recording method is entered on the chart.

Materials
The precise materials to be used in teaching are described on the chart. If a woolly toy is to be used, this would be unmistakeably identified, e.g. Georgina's blue teddy bear.

Place of work
The parent and teacher would decide where the teaching would take place.

That spot is described on the chart, e.g. on the floor in the living room, or Gary will be sitting in his moulded chair at his special table.

Directions
The words which will be used and how the skill will be demonstrated form the next part of the discussion. The two might act out the teaching session in order to be certain the directions are crystal clear. Once directions are agreed the parent may not use alternatives unless they are recorded and the parent can explain why the changes were made.

Success procedure
Most parents know what makes their child happy. It might be that the child loves to be cuddled. Some children are made happy by verbal praise like, "Well done, hey that's great". Others might love crisps or dolly mixtures. Whatever the parent believes will make the child feel good, and therefore aware, his mother is pleased and he is succeeding, is chosen and written down on the chart. E.g. If Sean eats all his cereal unaided Mummy will say "Well done, Sean" and bring him his favourite milk-shake. The aim of the success procedure is to make it clear to the child by praise or whatever that he has pleased his parent. This will make it more likely that the behaviour will be repeated.

Correction procedure
There are three strategies usually employed if the child either makes a mistake or will not co-operate. Almost certainly one of these correction procedures would be chosen:

a Verbal correction; telling the child he has made a mistake by pointing out where he went wrong and asking him to begin again.
b Modelling correct behaviour; showing the child how to complete the task correctly and asking him to repeat the behaviour after demonstration.
c Physical guidance; literally holding on to the child and guiding his limbs through the activity.

All these nine points which belong to the teaching framework are written down. As a result the parent can ensure that every teaching session will be exactly the same. Learning anything is easier if the teacher behaves consistently. If someone uses a number of ways to demonstrate a task, or sometimes encourages the child's efforts and sometimes does not, or sometimes forgets to correct errors, the learner can become confused. A golden rule of good teaching is to make a good plan and stick to it like glue.

If the child does not learn the skill, then it is relatively simple if this framework is used to analyse where the teaching plan was incorrectly designed. Failure to learn is usually the result of poor teaching!

The story of Selfish Sarah
The simplicity of these charts to make and their value to a teacher can be seen in the story of 'Selfish Sarah'. Everybody at some time has heard a parent call their child 'selfish', 'self-centered' or 'downright greedy'. These 'fuzzy' words are used to describe children who refuse to share their possessions with adults or other children. 'Selfishness' can bring both awkward and embarrassing results for adults. "I'm sorry Michael hit Tony with his train but you see he doesn't like sharing and Tony did try to take it away. I'm sorry Tony had to have three stitches but ...". Children produce some excellent strategies for avoiding sharing such as screaming, fighting, kicking, throwing full-scale tantrums, whining or running away.

Sarah was such a child. Her unwillingness to share had wrecked several children's tea parties, made life with her elder sister difficult and caused her parents distress. Her parents decided on a long-term

ACTIVITY CHART

Child's name **Sarah**

Starting date **Wed. 17th April.**

Teaching target **Sarah will share biscuits with an adult visitor when requested**

How often to practise
Twice a day (after lunch and after tea).

Success rate

2 out 2

What to record
Record results of each of two trials per day.

Materials **Two biscuits.**

Place of work **In the living room.**

Directions **Lead Sarah over to adult, who is seated, give Sarah two biscuits. Place one in each hand. Say "Now Sarah give.......a biscuit please" and gently touch her arm as you say this.**

Success procedure
If Sarah gives one biscuit to adult, say "well done, now you eat your biscuit," and let her eat the other biscuit.

Correction procedure
If Sarah attempts to eat the biscuit instead take her arm and gently guide it while she hands biscuit to seated adult. Say "That's a nice girl Sarah" and prime seated adult to praise her also.

How to record

✓ if Sarah gives biscuit without prompting.

Ⓥ if you have to help her.

(Graph)

Vertical axis: Teaching trials recorded each day — marked 1 and 2

Horizontal axis: Days of the week
Wed. Thurs. Fri. Sat. Sun. Mon. Tues. Wed.

Row at level 2: ✓ Ⓥ ✓ ✓ ✓ ✓ ✓ ✓

Row at level 1: Ⓥ Ⓥ ✓ ✓ ✓ ✓ ✓ ✓

goal of Sarah sharing sweets, toys and her crayons (which she kept under her bed and would let no one but her mother touch) with other children including those younger than herself. As a first step to a difficult target, her parents aimed for Sarah learning in one week to share biscuits from the biscuit tin with an adult visitor.

The Activity Chart drawn up by her parents is shown on page 73. You will see the nine steps resulting from preparation and planning are outlined.

The chart shows that by the third day she had achieved the success rate of two out of two. Her parents were pleased by her speedy success but quite correctly made her practise the skill for the next five days. All skills need to be practised before adults and children use them spontaneously. The chart also shows how the second day was bad for Sarah. She had to be helped on both occasions.

Bad days can bring teaching programmes to a grinding halt if records are not kept. Frequently parents tell us they have tried many different ways of changing behaviour. Without records when failure occurred, they changed their teaching plan. Parents scuttling around hunting for an alternative teaching strategy become inconsistent and poor teachers.

Careful recording has taught us that most people (adults as well as children) do not improve new behaviours a little more each day, but tend to have good and bad days. If you graph successes the result is an overall ascending success rate with an odd downward kink. Careful records to enable the parent to evaluate what is happening and after a period of time to see success.

Miles' chart

A second example of an effective use of activity charts is shown opposite for Miles. At age four, he was finding it difficult to speak. This chart is a small step belonging to a long language programme. Teaching a spoken language activity is more difficult than teaching many other skills. Few correction procedures are available apart from verbal prompting or showing the child what to do.

The teaching target chosen for Miles in the week shown was "Miles will name four pictures in a book when his mother points to them without a verbal prompt". The nine teaching points have been scrupulously adhered to on the chart. The correction procedure decided upon if Miles remained silent was that his mother would take his hand, guide it into a pointing position at the picture and say, "There is a

ACTIVITY CHART

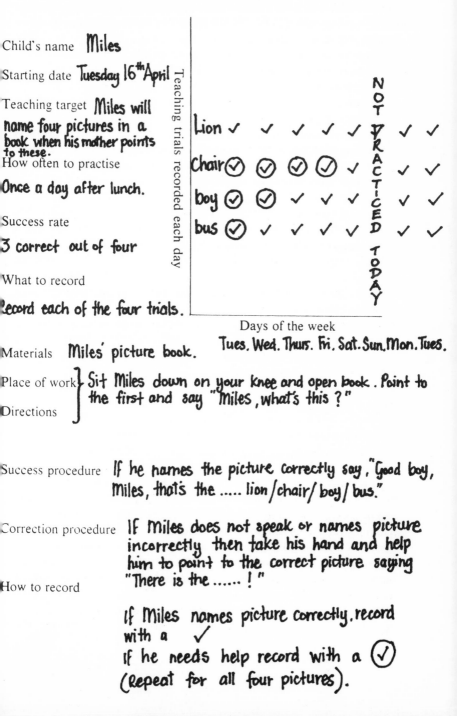

Child's name **Miles**

Starting date **Tuesday 16ᵗʰ April**

Teaching target **Miles will name four pictures in a book when his mother points to these.**

How often to practise

Once a day after lunch.

Success rate

3 correct out of four

What to record

Record each of the four trials.

Teaching trials recorded each day

	Tues.	Wed.	Thurs.	Fri.	Sat.	Sun.	Mon.	Tues.
Lion	✓	✓	✓	✓	✓	N O T	✓	✓
Chair	⊘	⊘	⊘	⊘	✓	P R A C T I C E D	✓	✓
boy	⊘	⊘	✓	✓	✓		✓	✓
bus	⊘	✓	✓	✓	✓	T O D A Y	✓	✓

Days of the week

Materials **Miles' picture book.**

Place of work ⎫
⎬ **Sit Miles down on your knee and open book. Point to the first and say "Miles, what's this?"**
Directions ⎭

Success procedure **If he names the picture correctly say, "Good boy, Miles, that's the ..... lion/chair/boy/bus."**

Correction procedure **If Miles does not speak or names picture incorrectly then take his hand and help him to point to the correct picture saying "There is the ...... !"**

How to record

**If Miles names picture correctly, record with a ✓
if he needs help record with a ⊘
(Repeat for all four pictures).**

bus/boy/chair or lion." The recording system shows Miles learned to name the lion, bus and boy by the third day but the chair took a little longer. The chart reflects that there were no practices on the Sunday because the family visited their grandparents. The lack of practice does not appear to have affected his learning as for the last two days of the week he was 100 per cent correct.

Another problem tackled using an activity chart was teaching a previously physically handicapped child to ride her bicycle unaided. The solution used is given on page 78 but the empty chart opposite is for you to work out a chart for the same activity – it might turn out a better strategy than the one which was used. The problem to overcome was to teach her to pedal and steer simultaneously.

Activity charts help parents to focus on selecting the best method for teaching a new skill or behaviour and even more important provide easy recording of progress. Such charts can be used by any parent of a young child or a child with special needs, to teach practically any skill.

Such charts are most useful in situations where adults have to make the decisions about what the child is going to learn. The child's role is usually that of a non-participant in all the decision making which precedes lessons. Parents or teachers state what is to be changed or learned and to what degree of skill. The pupil's role is reduced to that of a learner.

Charlie Charts

With older children there are many occasions where children and parents agree there is a need to learn new activities or behaviours. Once this happens and the pupil can begin to contribute to both preparation and planning stages, then there are other methods which can be used. Some elements of the preparation and planning stages remain mainly the province of the teacher.

Few children are able to see their own behaviour clearly enough to identify and define problems or to state target behaviours. But most can understand when these are explained carefully. By fourteen years old many teenagers can design a task analysis on their own. If an adult discusses a proposed teaching programme with their child then he is in a position to state what he feels he can achieve and to agree on performances. Many children know precisely what they can manage at each step.

With older children, the areas in which most alternative methods are available to the teacher are recording or monitoring of progress, the

ACTIVITY CHART

Child's name **Kate.**

Starting date **Wed. 17th April**

Teaching target **Kate will pedal her tricycle for three feet without any help.**

How often to practise

Success rate

What to record

Teaching trials recorded each day

Days of the week

Materials

Place of work

Directions

Success procedure

Correction procedure

How to record

ACTIVITY CHART

Child's name **Kate**

Starting date **Wed 17th April.**

Teaching target **Kate will pedal her tricycle for three feet without any help.**

How often to practise
3 times each day.

Success rate
2 out of 3.

What to record
Record results of first two teaching trials each day only.

Materials **Kate's bike**

Place of work **Sit Kate on her bike in the lounge.**

Directions **Place her feet on the pedals of the fixed wheel. Give her a little push and say "You pedal, Kate."**

Success procedure **If Kate pedals for approx. 3 feet, say "Well done, what a clever girl you are". and give her a hug.**

Correction procedure **If she does not pedal push her feet down on the pedals to help her. Praise her as the bike moves.**

How to record

✓ If Kate pedals by herself.

⊘ If you have to push her feet down.

Teaching trials recorded each day

2 — ⊘ ⊘ ⊘ ⊘ ⊘ ✓ ✓

1 — ⊘ ⊘ ⊘ ⊘ ✓ ✓ ⊘

Days of the week
Wed. Thurs. Fri. Sat. Sun. Mon. Tues. We

recognition of succéss and correction procedures and making sure the successes are properly celebrated.

Charlie Charts are now featured in many classrooms. A Charlie Chart is usually a pictorial representation of a child's progress which can be hung on the wall for all to see. (Examples of these charts can be seen in the illustrations on pages 80, 82 and 88.)

Such a chart is usually made by a teacher or sometimes a parent after a discussion with the child concerned about the problem behaviour. The preparation and planning stage is sometimes completed with the child, but certainly is always discussed. Over the age of six years or so most children have a fair idea of how their behaviour is affecting others and can become usefully involved in planning changes. The criterion for the behaviour, the length of time the child would be expected to perform in a certain way or the number of times per day he should practise the skill, can all be agreed between adult and child. The length of time before the new behaviour is established can also be negotiated.

Charlie Charts are highly individualised and the design is associated with something in which the child is particularly interested or with the precise skill or behaviour he is going to try to change. A system of recording by marking the chart, and the precise time periods when this should occur are agreed in advance. The description of the desired behaviour is written on the chart in simple language together with all other essential information. If a behaviour needs a lengthy statement this might be written on the back, in full, for reference while the front contains a simple statement.

These charts, while performing the same role as an activity chart, have several useful spin-offs. The child is clear about the behaviour which is expected of him. He can see at a glance what is his success rate, he can show the chart to his friends, uncles, aunts, and a complete stranger, each of whom are instantly aware of his achievement. A Charlie Chart has a limited life but limitless possibilities.

Sam was a monster

There was a small boy called Sam who because of his extreme behaviours earned himself a description of being 'maladjusted' before he was six years old. In class his particular problems related to an inability to stay in his seat working on a topic for more than five minutes without approaching the teacher, pushing and shoving other children out of his way to reach the teacher, and destroying other children's work. Once the whole class laboriously painted blown eggs

for Easter, and at breaktime Sam sneaked back in to the classroom and stamped on each and every one. In the playground he was often involved in fights. He had difficulty with all his schoolwork.

Here are the teacher's notes!

Sam, Class 1

Good points –
1 Helpful to younger children, especially when they fall over, get bumped in the playground, etc.
2 Drawing, colouring and painting is good. Can work on his own at these activities.
3 Will play with model cars with another child for up to half an hour at a time.

Problems –
1 Is out of his seat about 75 per cent of the time.
2 Pushes other children who get in his way.
3 Damages (tears or scribbles over) other children's work.
4 Fights with older boys at playtime.
5 Cannot copy simple words from the blackboard.
6 Cannot sight read more than ten simple words.
7 Will sneakily destroy special things left in class when everyone is outside.

Priority problem –
Out of seat more than 75 per cent of the time.

Desired outcome –
Sam will remain in his seat except when told by me that he can leave, e.g. toilet, classroom activities, etc., or after raising hand to ask permission to leave.

Possible steps –
1 Remain in seat for two half-hour sessions (a.m. and p.m. each day).
2 Remain in seat for four half-hour sessions each day.
3 Remain in seat except when told he can leave seat.

Teaching target –
Sam will remain in seat for four half-hour lessons (two a.m., two p.m.), carry out class assignment, raising hand if he needs help.

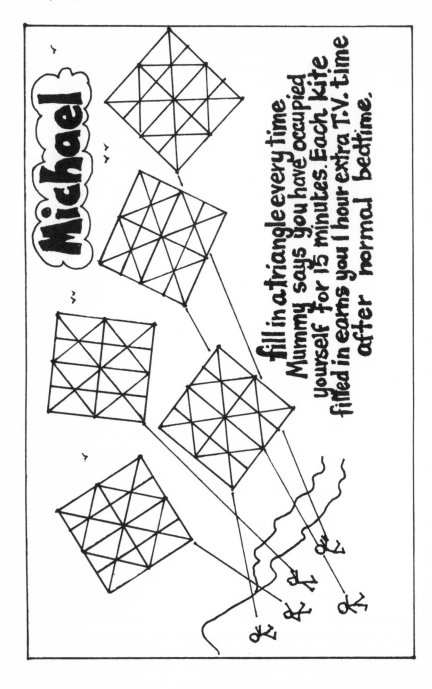

The teacher decided the priority problem was Sam's habit of leaving his seat and repeatedly approaching her for attention. It was at these times that he became involved in barging and shouting and generally making the class uncomfortable. She made a Charlie Chart showing a race track divided into tiny sections. In discussion with Sam it was agreed that during each of four half-hour lessons, for each ten minutes he remained in his seat, raising his hand if he wanted help and working as instructed, he could move his car (which he painted black) along one section, which would be coloured in. If he was 'bad', he could move the car but not colour the section. He could earn bonus sections for particularly good behaviour. The criteria for staying in his seat were minutely discussed: did it apply during story time, music and dance, etc? The rules were written out in full on the back and more cryptically on the front. The class were told Sam was trying to behave differently and the chart after explanation put up on the wall. The chart showed the days of the week split into periods. In seconds the teacher could spot Sam's good and bad days by seeing where the track had not been coloured. This chart had a life of four weeks. In that time, Sam changed his behaviour completely and to make sure it stayed changed, a maintenance programme was initiated. A second Charlie Chart was designed to help him maintain his good behaviour for a complete morning at school.

If another psychologist or teacher had told us this story two or three years ago we might well have not believed it to be true. In fact Sam is a real boy and now two years later he has transferred to another Junior School. (His parents moved house.) His good behaviour is continuing. Why?

The answer will be explained in more detail later in the book. The important things to recognise in this story are that at the beginning Sam was focusing attention on himself for a major portion of each day. Children and teacher alike were forced to respond to him in a nasty way because his behaviour was so awful. But he was a 'somebody' in the class. There are advantages to being an outlaw as well as a good guy. Everybody notices an outlaw!

Sam's background left a lot to be desired. After many rows and much violence his father and mother divorced when he was four years old. His mother plus her four children moved to another town. She was rehoused by the Council and given social security benefits on which she raised her children. When Sam was four she stated that he was "hurtful, deceitful and aggressive and just like his father". She said she knew she should not "take out all her hurt and anger on Sam" but that she knocked him around and often sent him to his room. Sam was the child she deprived of treats and spoiling and when first in Infants School there was a marked difference in his physically cared for condition than that of his sister and brother.

When Sam was nearly six she began living with a 'kind and gentle' man approximately fifteen years younger. Sam continued to be difficult at home and his mother sought help from social services. That brings us near to the time when the Charlie Chart began. A meeting was held at which Sam's behaviour was discussed between head-teacher, class teacher, mother, step-father and psychologist.

The psychologist suggested that Sam's bad behaviour related to his 'need for attention and constant reassurance from his teacher'. The Charlie Chart contents were discussed and also his mother gave permission for a correction procedure to be used when he was naughty. This was that Sam would be removed from class and taken to the school medical room – a stark, bare, boring room – and there left for ten minutes.

It was agreed that every time this sanction was used it would be recorded and his mother informed. Both parents agreed to notice when Sam behaved well at home and tell him so – even if it was very little like saying 'please'.

What happened to Sam when the chart began was that suddenly his little world turned upside down. When he was bad, which before had been good for ten minutes of clear attention and maybe a chat with the teacher or even the Head, earned him ten minutes in that miserable hole of a medical room and no chats or attention. When he conformed he was regularly told how good he was being and the class as well as the teacher paid him attention. As the psychologist involved it was highly gratifying walking into the classroom two weeks after the chart began and idly asking a child what the chart meant. "That's Sam's," came the reply. "It shows he's being good." "Wasn't he always good?" "He is now."

Sam was taught by the class and teacher that he *gained more* by being good than naughty. Gradually the attention he received for good behaviour was reduced over a period of time but by then he no longer resorted to disruptive behaviour to become the centre of attention.

His mother proved herself highly successful at encouraging him at home and the end result was successful for everyone, especially Sam.

Contracts

A third major teaching aid which is becoming popular with older children, is 'the contract'. Charlie Charts are great fun for small children, but once adolescents are involved a more adult approach is required. Like the chart, the contract fulfils the function of an *aide-mémoire*, it contains all the criteria for practice and success, it defines when, where and how the behaviour will be completed and it states any agreed reinforcement for success. On both chart and contract the success and correction procedures are clearly defined. As both are meant to be positive aids often the success procedure will be permission to do something the person enjoys and the correction procedure deprivation of that or another agreed privilege.

Revision: Performing

To perform the teaching task successfully you must:
1 Make sure you have completed all the elements of the preparation and planning stages.
2 Stick consistently to your teaching plan.
3 Direct, lead, encourage and correct pupil's performance.
4 Practise the skill until learned.
5 Record progress.

Aids to successful teaching:
1 An Activity Chart when the teacher makes all the decisions or
2 A Charlie Chart to involve an older child or
3 A Contract with older children, adolescents and adults where joint negotiation takes place.

The contract on page 86 was worked out after a lot of discussion and most of the ideas came from Freddie himself. A chart[5] on page 88 was made on which the score could be kept, and Freddie hung it over his bed. The important elements in this contract are that it is specific in its requirements, giving examples of what to do and what not to do. Also, provision is made for temporary failure on the programme, or complete failure. One of the main advantages of contract formulation, with heavy emphasis on the child's personal involvement, is that if it does

[5] Further information on contracts appears in Burland, J. R. (1979) 'Behaviour Modification in a Residential School for Junior Maladjusted Boys: A Review', *Journal of the Association of Workers for Maladjusted Children*. Vol. 7, No. 2. Autumn.

I, Freddie, agree to be helpful with others in my class (e.g. sharing my comics and toys, being nice to other boys, being a good example by following instructions) and will not disturb other boys by teasing them, taking their belongings, calling them names, or getting in their way. I will be able to earn two points in the morning and two points in the afternoon if I am helpful, but if I do any unhelpful things I agree that I should be put on Time Out. When I reach a total of 36 points earned, I can be allowed to buy 70 pence worth of fishing tackle from the Rod Shop. If this contract does not work in some way I agree to it being changed.

Signed..............Freddie

.................Teacher

Date.....................

not work out it is a technical problem rather than a personal one, and it is 'back to the drawing board' to effect a more efficient contract. No party need feel let down, or that they are letting someone else down.

Points to ponder
Teaching a new skill successfully, whatever that skill may be, from learning to read and write, to eating with a spoon unaided, or riding a bicycle, or making one's own bed and tidying one's bedroom daily, is dependent on the teacher putting the right components into the programme.

The teacher's tasks relate to identifying the behaviour, defining it, analysing the sub-skills underlying the activity and constructing a logical teaching programme. The pupil's tasks relate to (1) perceiving what is required as the new behaviour (2) being able to perform the behaviour and (3) wanting to do so.

The first of these last three can be made simple if the teacher and pupil have discussed and agreed the level of difficulty of the activity. The second is often a matter of sheer practice with or without a teacher at hand to achieve perfection. The third point is the trickiest to control. People want to do things in a different way and learn new skills if by so doing good things happen for them. Those good things might be a part of the task itself, such as the pleasure of having done something well or mastering some new skill bringing personal satisfaction. With children, those good things more often relate to external factors, adults noticing change, brothers and sisters being congratulatory, other children being nicer, or being rewarded with pocket money for doing chores, sweets for good behaviour or maybe something long desired as a reward for outstanding effort: a bicycle, camera or watch. In all human endeavour there is a pay-off, whether material, like a wage packet, or less tangible like social acclaim or personal satisfaction. If there is neither recognition by others, nor inner satisfaction, it is highly unlikely the activity will be repeated. The teacher may have to teach but no child has to try to learn – but the teacher can induce that desire by building in a reward. The simplest of all is perhaps a smile and yet also perhaps the most effective.

A Charlie Chart and Contract provide mechanical aids to make sure the person striving after a new behaviour is appropriately noticed, reinforced and rewarded positively for effort. It is a common failing to notice the bad and criticise while letting the good pass by unremarked. On the whole people are not very good at telling others when they have

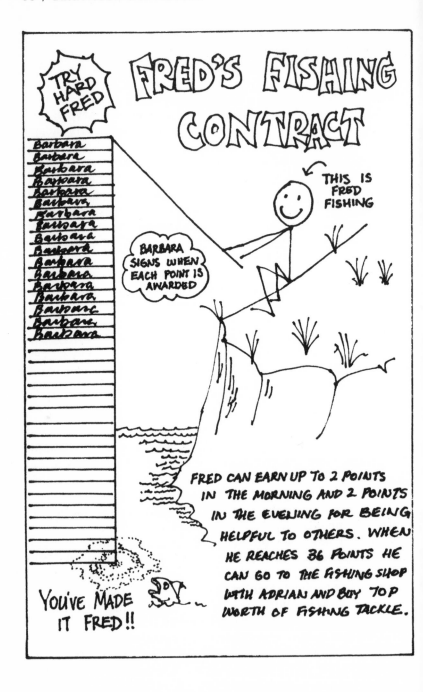

done well. Just think how many compliments you have received today or this week! Or conversely think how many times you have been criticised already today! The use of a good recording system enables this positive commenting to become natural and it makes it far easier for teacher and taught to experience mutual success.

The Activity Chart is the purest method of demonstrating the nine point teaching programme. The Charlie Chart and Contract can be used with great effect as positive teaching aids, which have as their foundation the nine point framework.

Finally, there are situations in life where adults recognise problems which they or their working or marriage partners are facing. Within the context of a relationship where people have learned to share responsibility there is the opportunity for complete joint decision making. It is possible to define problems clearly and to agree targets for change and then to follow the planning and performing stages.

Often adults do agree certain changes but do not build into those agreements the necessary ingredients for recognising another's good efforts, their success and their progress. These are vital ingredients of a successful venture to change behaviour.

Behaviour can change no matter the age or the length of time it has continued or the apparent tendency of the person concerned to slip back into bad habits. Adhering to the elements of the three 'Ps' of successful teaching is the easiest way to make good changes happen. Remember – preparation, planning and performing!

6

Seeing is believing

Observation and the reasons for data collection

Periodically psychologists try to evaluate the service they render to teachers and parents. The usual methods they use in their evaluations are questionnaires or surveys.

Such enquiries tell us teachers regard psychologists as useful in two main areas. Firstly it is the psychologist who often gives advice on the best teaching programmes or even alternative schools for children who have unique learning problems. Secondly, psychologists help teachers to deal with children's problem behaviour. Teachers say they notice psychologists adopt a scientific approach.

We suggest that what psychologists do (and are able to teach others to do) is how to observe behaviour objectively. Psychologists highlight exactly what is sustaining the problem. Outline a problem clearly and you are already half way to solving it!

In order to change behaviour, the person causing the problems must either be taught a new way to behave or helped to unlearn the behaviour. It is difficult to begin if the people wanting change are 'fuzzy' about the problem.

Have you ever thought how easy it is to misinterpret behaviour? Or what poor witnesses we are to what goes on around us?

There is the sad story of the furniture salesman who made a buying trip to London from the provinces. While there he met a French girl who knew few words of English. His French was even more limited. Through gesture and the odd word they communicated. At last he drew a knife, fork and plate on a card. She nodded enthusiastically and they dined together. Much later as the candles guttered low on the table and they gazed into each others eyes, she drew a bed on her napkin. "How on earth," he asked his friends at work next day, "did she know I was in the furniture business?" History does not relate whether she made her meaning clear in the end.

Good observation combined with the proper use of the ABC of behaviour equals good interventions and strategies for helping behaviour to change. Jack's story shows the use of observation.

Jack was referred to our service by his class teacher. She complained he was "aggressive"; persistently involved in fights in class. As he was reported never to fight during playtime or at lunch, we suggested a period of observation in the classroom. The teacher agreed to two psychology students observing Jack's behaviour.

With clipboards at the ready, stop-watches and charts, the two arrived one morning and settled down in the classroom trying to be as unobtrusive as possible. By breaktime the class had become quite used to their presence and were reverting to normal behaviour.

Jack was given his maths exercise to complete. He began to work as did the rest of the class. Dutifully the students noted his 'on task' behaviour on their charts during the next twenty minutes.

He finished his work. He picked up his pencil and book and walked to the teacher's desk where there was a considerable queue of children waiting to have their sums marked. A couple of minutes later, another boy, Richard, joined the group and pushed past two children to stand next to Jack. He began to push and nudge Jack who ignored him. He pushed harder, Jack moved away. As the students watched fascinated, Richard picked up a red crayon from the desk and deliberately scribbled on Jack's book. In a flash, Jack turned and thumped the boy. He punched him hard and knocked Richard to the floor. The teacher leapt up from the desk, grabbed both boys by the nearest bit of their anatomy, swung them towards the students and cried, "Do you see what I mean, he's a little devil." She took Jack by the arm and thrust him protesting out of the room.

What did the period of observation demonstrate? This is where the ABC of behaviour becomes useful. First look at the *antecedent events*: immediately before the fight, Richard deliberately scribbled on Jack's book. Before that, Jack had withstood or ignored several less irritating but provoking actions from Richard. If we look back further in time,

Jack had been behaving quite peacefully. He had been working hard. Jack had at no time behaved in a way which suggested that he was looking for a fight. His 'aggressions' occurred only when severely provoked.

Did the *background* contribute to the incident? The teacher who was busily marking books was totally obscured from view by the queue of children. She was taking care over her marking and thus children were standing in the queue for some time. Just as the children could not see the teacher, they knew she could not see them. Anybody feeling bored and like a little naughtiness, could behave badly, predicting they would not be caught. Almost certainly, the background played an important part in the incident. The teacher had unwittingly provided a setting or situation in which Jack could be both provoked and retaliate. The other children in the class would be able to predict from his past behaviour that Jack would lose his temper quickly. He became – once he joined that jostling queue – fair game!

Finally, were the *consequences*, the teacher's reaction and being pushed out of class likely to help Jack to keep his temper in future? It could be argued that the teacher was in fact acting in a way which would suggest to Jack he was being 'picked on', unfairly punished and not given a chance to explain or have a 'just' hearing. If this was the case, then the teacher's behaviour was probably making it more likely for Jack to misbehave in the future.

She had not looked at his work which he had completed and which deserved to be marked. Jack had not been complimented for doing the right thing. Instead he was thrust out of class and humiliated in front of his friends and two strangers. Do you think that these consequences would make him want to go on trying to please his teacher?

In this example, Jack's fighting, when scrutinised, turns out to be almost legitimate. Who among us would not have responded with a degree of anger if so provoked? The antecedent events were directly responsible for the incident. But could the teacher have prevented them happening by organising the classroom differently? Was her behaviour after the incident (the consequences) likely to help Jack stay out of fights?

What happened was that the students as tactfully and diplomatically as possible explained to the teacher what they had observed. She found it difficult to believe Jack had been provoked. She had never seen him immediately before an incident. The students suggested re-arranging

the background in which the behaviour had occurred as a first step towards changing Jack's behaviour. The teacher reluctantly agreed to change her system of marking work. Instead of sitting at her desk and children coming to her, she asked the children to put their hands up when they had finished and she moved from desk to desk.

This system had two by-products. The teacher could see most of her class at any time and began to observe the behaviour of her pupils more closely. Her assessments of children's behaviour became more accurate. She saw what happened and apportioned blame fairly. Secondly, she noticed, unprompted by the students, how much 'do nothing' time they experienced while waiting for their work to be marked.

To tackle this problem she devised a simple system which involved changing antecedents. When giving the children a work assignment, she began giving them a second task to complete which was entirely different: a maths exercise followed by reading or a written assignment followed by drawing. By having a different exercise as the second assignment she could pick out the children who had finished the first piece of work and moved to them quickly without even the need for them to put their hands up. Secondly, she said she discovered children worked more happily if after they had completed a piece of work which required concentrated effort, they had a short period of less demanding activity before moving on to the next taxing assignment.

In this particular case of using an ABC approach, it was found that the antecedent, Jack being provoked by Richard, was mainly controlling the unwanted behaviour. But the behaviour would probably not have occurred in a different background. Consequences, too, were playing their part. The case demonstrates also how tactful anyone has to be when they become involved in the 'observing game'.

Before it is possible to devise strategies or consider the types of intervention which will cause people to unlearn behaviour, be it adult behaviour like smoking, or child behaviour like tantrums, it is necessary to know how to observe behaviours in order to decide which elements under the heading A, B or C are maintaining the behaviour.

How to observe
Observation requires objectivity and it is tough trying to be objective about our own behaviour or those close around us. The best kind of observation is that completed by someone who is not a member of the family or the class involved.

In the school setting one of the most useful people to co-opt as an observer in class, or the playground, is the school secretary or, perhaps, a non-teaching assistant. Such people are well known to the children and on a variety of occasions would be visiting classrooms anyway. Moreover the teachers accept their presence in class as 'neutral'. Teachers can be made quite uncomfortable if observed by other trained personnel. Not surprising, as most of us dislike being watched by other professionals who may be unnecessarily critical. As the idea is to observe the whole setting as naturally as possible it is more sensible to find an impartial observer who will cause little anxiety to teacher or class. Non-teaching assistants and school secretaries can find ten minutes every so often to observe, given that the headteacher can spare their services for short periods.

Supposing a child is reported to be utterly charming, and helpful in school, but constantly out of seat, not working when told, interfering with others and trying to attract too much teacher attention. The teacher might long for the child to learn to stay in his chair, complete work assignments and to leave her and the other children in peace. She might want to know:

a What events occurred before the poor behaviour (antecedents).
b Whether they occurred in some situations and not in others (background).
c What effect her reaction and those of the class had on the behaviour (consequences).
d The frequency.

Frequency has not been mentioned before. It has important implications for accepting behaviours. A behaviour deficit or excess cause problems because they occur too often or too rarely. Something like cracking your finger joints may not matter if it happens say twice a fortnight. Believe it, if someone continuously cracks their joints it is a real problem.

Obviously, one period of observation is not going to produce all the answers to the questions. Equally obviously, no school secretary or non-teaching assistant has the time to sit in a classroom for extended periods. A solution is for such people to agree to visit the classroom once each morning and again in the afternoon to observe for ten minutes. At the end of a week the child would have been observed for a total of a hundred minutes spread over five days. These observations would cover different lessons and times of day. From that amount of information, patterns emerge which provide answers to teacher's questions.

Successful observation is *selective observation*. No one other than a shorthand expert or film cameraman can record all the actions of one person in ten minutes accurately. It is wise, therefore, to choose

specific aspects to observe. One way is to make a chart with time periods blocked on the vertical axis and the things to be observed along the horizontal axis. In this case the secretary wrote the lesson and time period across the top. She checked whether the child was 'on task' or 'off task', 'in' or 'out' of seat, attracting teacher or class attention and receiving teacher or class attention at one minute intervals. The secretary also wrote in little supplementary notes as an *aide-mémoire* to make the observation clearer when looked at a week later.

In this particular case the teacher on checking the chart decided there was evidence to suggest:

a The child was most disruptive when sitting with one other boy and during maths lessons when he appeared to spend more time playing with and tossing around equipment than working.
b He was involved in 'off task' behaviour considerably less than she had previously supposed.
c He did not respond to teacher attention when misbehaving by subsequently behaving appropriately.

Looking at the evidence collected in terms of our ABC, she estimated that some of the behaviour of which she complained related to the antecedent and background events. She decided to ensure the boy was separated from the other child with whom he was often in trouble. She looked at the maths programme she had given the boy to work on and decided it was too easy for him. She worked out a new and more suitable maths curriculum.

This teacher was bemused by the evidence that her pupil appeared to be less well behaved after corrective teacher attention. The psychologist suggested that this might relate to the fact that he always gained attention when misbehaving. She worked out from the chart what was the child's average length of 'on task' behaviour. She decided to speak encouragingly to him just before his average time limit of work expired.

Happily the techniques she employed were successful and the boy became 'on task' more often, and less disruptive. Not all schools have teachers as analytic in their approach as this one, nor compliant secretaries who will sit taking observations. So sometimes it is necessary for a teacher to take her own observations.

Observing in school

This can be achieved in several ways, but perhaps the easiest is to bring a household oven timer into class and tell the children the timer will ring at odd intervals in the day. An alternative to a timer is the micro chip pocket calculator with a built-in alarm buzzer which can be used for timings.

Armed with a clipboard and chart, which shows time on the vertical axis and activities under observation on the horizontal axis, the teacher sets the timer for an interval of time, e.g. ten minutes. When it rings she notes what the child under observation is doing in terms of her selected criteria with a neat tick. She resets the timer for a *different* length of time and so on throughout the day.

Children, strangely enough, react well to such experiments finding it quite amusing to have the timer operating for a few days. It is not difficult for the teacher or too disruptive of her time, and she can accumulate a considerable amount of useful information relatively swiftly. At the end of a few days she will have a number of little probes of behaviour which she can then interpret in terms of ABC.

Older children in secondary school when involved in trying to change their own behaviour have been known to use the timer technique for self-observation. One boy found it difficult to work for prolonged periods. His teachers and he were of the opinion that he was 'daydreaming' for at least half of each lesson. He was provided with a timer and a chart listing varied or random time periods. He was instructed to set the timer, place it on the floor and when it rang, note what he was doing before resetting the timer and starting work again. Interestingly enough no other intervention was necessary. Within a day he had demonstrated to himself and to staff that he could work for extended periods.

Observation makes for accurate assessment of behaviour

Within school settings it is common for teachers to see so many pieces of poor behaviour from a child that they almost begin to expect him to behave all the time in a disruptive manner. Observation in schools is a basic step towards changing behaviour. It is hard trying to change a behaviour without establishing why it can happen. It is also fairly impossible trying to change alleged behaviour without checking to see if it is occurring. It is not unusual to find people complaining of behaviours long after the child has stopped exhibiting them or believing a child does something more frequently than is in fact the case.

A typical experience is summed up by the case of Sean. He was a six-year-old given to explosive tantrums when thwarted. In the initial interview, the parent and teacher agreed he was throwing tantrums between three and five times a day. Some of these would be at school. Both negotiated to note the 'A' antecedent events to a tantrum, 'B' the background and the extent of the behaviour and 'C' the consequences of the behaviour. Under 'C' was to be noted what they did to stop the behaviour and the boy's reactions. Finally, they agreed to note what he was doing ten minutes later.

In fact a week's observation showed that he threw only two tantrums, one at home in the evening and one on the same day at the school sports. Both adults were amazed and expressed the opinion that these results were a 'fluke'. They elected to keep note the following week. Again the number of tantrums was two, both in school and spaced by three days!

Another incidence of this type of exaggeration of other people's failings concerned a boy in a residential school who was 'disorganised'. The staff, among other irritations, were angered by the way he never had his pens, paper or books for lessons. His tutor suggested that if this behaviour could be corrected, it would take the pressure off him and the staff.

All the staff who taught him elected to note before each lesson whether he had his things. At the beginning of the week he was reminded what equipment he should bring to each lesson. He was not told the staff were checking on him. Each staff member kept their own notes and handed them to the headteacher who collated the results of the observations. At the ensuing staff meeting, the Head's statement that there had only been one occasion within the week when he had not had his kit was met with universal disbelief.

It is the most human of human failings to say someone 'always does something' because he has done it a number of times. The expression 'give a dog a bad name' is an accurate description of what can happen. A person can be dogged by his reputation of 'behaving badly' long after the behaviour has ceased to exist. This is especially true in any organisation where contact occurs infrequently but regularly between people such as in a large school. A teacher in a comprehensive school might see a child only once a week and be responding to the child's reputed rather than his actual behaviour. Hence the need for observation!

Observing at home

Problem behaviour at home can be observed by using frequency counts, by specially designed charts or by the simplest and most behaviour specific method: recording precisely what happened when the behaviour occurred. Selective observation is still the rule; do not try to record too much. Decide which behaviour (or maybe two behaviours) will be recorded. Design a chart or sheet which will enable you to record the five following bits of information:

1 The behaviour: what happened, who was involved, what inanimate objects were used (if any at all), e.g. a brick through the kitchen window!

2 The antecedent events: what was going on before the behaviour occurred, or were the antecedent events separated in time from the actual behaviour? E.g. the children are playing cowboys and Indians in the garden. They eat tea. Later Dad is sitting reading a paper and asking for quiet and the children renew their game, this time in the house. Dad loses his temper, the children are excitable, one bursts into tears and the situation escalates into a full-scale row. The antecedents to the row would not be simply Dad losing his temper. The antecedents relate to the period when the children were letting off steam in the garden, the enforced quietness of tea and their desire to continue the game.

3 The background or the setting in which the behaviour occurred.

4 The consequences of the behaviour: pleasant things which occurred or the punishment, and the responses of everyone involved in the situation.

5 The aftermath: what was the situation ten or maybe thirty minutes after the event had occurred? Had the behaviour been terminated, had the situation returned to normal, or were people still arguing, etc?

Opposite is a record kept by a mother for one week. Her son Matthew was reported as a screamer. His mother summed it up by saying "Matthew would shout and scream over nothing". Looking at the records, it appears these events occurred whenever Matthew was asked to do something he did not want to do or, when someone took

PROBLEM: Matthew lies down on the floor and kicks and screams 2–3 times per day.

THE BEHAVIOUR – What did Matthew do?	ANTECEDENTS – i.e. What do you think provoked it?	BACKGROUND – i.e. Where did it happen?	CONSEQUENCES – i.e. What did you do to stop it?	THE AFTERMATH – What happened as a result of your efforts?
MONDAY Lay down on the floor and screamed. Lay down on the floor and kicked.	Bill took one of his lorries. I said "Matthew clear away all your toys into the toy box."	In the living room after he came home from school. In the living room just before bedtime.	Told him to go into the garden until he felt better. I ignored him and went to make myself a coffee.	He stopped screaming after five minutes. He stopped screaming and kicking after ten minutes. It could have been longer.
TUESDAY Screamed and banged on the kitchen floor. Screamed and banged hard on the hall door.	Usual thing! Bill and Matthew wanted the same toy. I called him to come in from the garden one of the rain.	In the afternoon about ½ hour later in the garden.	Sent them both to the garden to cool off. I sent him to bed. I'd had enough by then.	Couldn't really stay, they stopped very soon, say 3 til 4 minutes later. Stopped after about 5 minutes and then came downstairs O.K.
WEDNESDAY Screamed and tried to hit Bill.	Bill broke his school pencil.	At the table in the living room.	gave Bill a telling off and gave Matthew a hug.	The screaming went on for about 5 to 6 minutes.
THURSDAY Screamed and kicked me on the ankle. It hurt too!	I said he couldn't sit too near the fire.	After school while I made his tea.	I got cross and turned off the fire.	It lasted for almost a quarter of an hour. I thought it was for ever.
FRIDAY Shouted and kicked on the piano.	Bill and Matthew were figuring about something which I can't remember.	In the living room just before bedtime.	Put both to bed and said I would read a story when the noise stopped.	I was amazed when I came up 5 minutes later Matthew was quiet and Bill was already asleep.
SATURDAY Matthew went fishing with his dad all day. He was as good as gold. But what a week I've had!!	—	—	—	—

something he wanted (the antecedents). Almost invariably these events occurred in the evening, after school and in the living room (the background). His mother reacted in a number of different ways. Her most successful intervention was sending both Matthew and his brother to bed and promising a story as a reward if they were quiet.

There is here, a wealth of information which would help a mother or father or both parents to analyse what made Matthew likely to explode and several ways to prevent this happening. The analysis might be even simpler if an outsider who was objective could also be involved.

So to help someone unlearn a behaviour, first you need to know just what happenings make it likely for the behaviour to appear. This knowledge can only be gained through careful objective observations. As we have shown there are several ways observation can be made easier and a few of these have been outlined.

Ain't life complicated?

We discovered observing our own behaviour closely could be a daunting experience. When we started applying the ABC, we learned that sometimes the way we were trying to change behaviours was actually making them more likely to occur again.

It is thoroughly uncomfortable for anyone to face the fact that the very way they are trying to change a habit may make it more likely to be repeated.

The salutary tale of sad Anna

Ian, one of our teacher colleagues, had a girl in his class whom he knew was experiencing considerable problems at home. Her parents were in the middle of a messy divorce. She did not know which parent she would eventually live with, although her brothers had already been told that they would live with her father. Not unnaturally, this eleven-year-old was tearful and one day cried pitiously during the lesson before break. Ian kept her behind during break and talked to her. He listened to her distraught story and tried to comfort her; apparently successfully as she ceased to cry.

A few days later it happened again. He repeated his role of comforter. Before long the child had been referred to the school psychologist because she cried persistently. What had been considered originally as a normal and natural reaction to a most unpleasant real life situation had become a problem. Her crying disrupted the class, prevented Ian from enjoying his short breaks in the staff room and caused anxious comments from senior staff.

When the psychologist applied the ABC rule, it appeared that there was no pattern of events which led up to the tears. Anna, who was normally a quiet girl, would just begin to cry and her next door neighbour would say something like, "Sir, Anna's crying again". The behaviour was always the same, the great tears rolling down her cheeks, resting her head on her arms, snuffling and squeaking. The rest of the class would gather around solicitously and Ian would promptly move to her side saying comforting things. He would tell her to sit quietly and not to worry about her work. As soon as break occurred, he would stay with her and talk and let her literally cry on his shoulder.

The school psychologist asked, "What do you think would happen if you took her out of the room, say to the medical room?" Ian said that would be cruel. The psychologist suggested that she might find it easier to stop crying on her own, in solitude. He pointed out that when someone is in floods of tears it is difficult for them to understand anything anyone says to them anyway. The teacher saw the sense of the argument, remembering that in his own case when involved in arguments he chose to withdraw to a quiet area. Once he was calm and had collected his thoughts, he would return and sort out the problem. Ian agreed therefore that 'B' the background might have a controlling influence on Anna's crying.

The psychologist accepted that Anna needed the cosy chat sessions and discussions of her problems. They gave her a chance to talk about the things which worried her with a caring, fairly objective adult.

The psychologist suggested that the outbreaks of crying were continuing because nice consequences resulted. She was always allowed to stop working, she received a lot of sympathy from her friends, and her teacher spent quite lengthy periods with her alone. Ian agreed that when she cried he would ask one of the older children in his class to take her to the medical room. He would tell Anna to come back into class as soon as she had stopped crying and could go on working. Anna's escort would be asked to tell the headteacher what had occurred before returning immediately to class. The reason for doing this was part of the plan. The headteacher had undertaken to peep into the medical room after about five minutes to make sure that Anna was not malingering.

The changes suggested by the psychologist in ABC terms are shown on page 104:

Events Surrounding Behaviour	From	To
A (antecedents)	no change	
B (background)	classroom	medical room
C (consequences)	friend's and teacher's attention for crying.	no attention given for crying but opportunities to discuss problem with teacher at agreed times.

The psychologist predicted that Anna would not remain away from class very long as, without the attention of her school friends and teachers, the crying would be more difficult to maintain. Time proved him right.

Ian agreed that there would be more chance of Anna's behaviour changing if the discussions of her problems did not occur immediately after a crying bout. Anna was offered the opportunity of coming into class early. He had a rule that no one could come in before the bell went, as he used that time to prepare work. Anna was made an exception to that rule and if she wanted she could pop in and talk to him as he worked.

Everyone agreed that the discussions were of great importance to Anna and must be maintained. But it was also agreed that at other periods like breaktime, if she tried to keep her teacher's attention, he would tell her that he was required to do something with another staff member or the headteacher, but he could see her at a specific time before afternoon school or morning school the next day. This arrangement allowed Ian to keep the control over ABC events in his hands and not allow Anna to manipulate him by her emotional behaviour.

What happened next followed an almost classic pattern of events. The next time Anna became distressed, she was taken to the medical room as planned. She was back in class within fifteen minutes and working. Later in the day there was another outburst. The treatment was repeated. Just before home time she burst into tears again. Once more she was escorted out of class. Ian kept her back after school for a moment or two and offered her the chance of seeing him in the morning and talking. She took it. The next day there were two more outbursts. The following day she saw him again, but although once or twice during the day the teacher thought she was about to cry, she did not. Over the next week the crying in class ended completely. Anna saw her teacher before school and when on occasion she began to sniffle, he handed her his handkerchief and told her he would leave her for a moment or two to compose herself.

It worked! Before long, Anna was talking rationally about her family and relating to the teacher in a different way. There were still odd occasions when she cried, but these became isolated incidents. Each directly related to specific upheavals like the day her parents went to court and when she and her mother left the marital home. The crying was no longer being maintained by the background or consequences, which occurred in the class, but occurred naturally because of antecedent events at home.

Ian had been asked to keep a record of Anna's tears. He had a diary in which he daily noted work completed by the class or any other special events. At the end of the first week he sent the school psychologist the following notes:

Teacher's notes on sad Anna. Results of new programme to deal with Anna's crying.

Day 1	10.00 a.m.	cried for 15 minutes	
	12.15 p.m.	cried for 10 minutes	3 occasions
	3.30 p.m.	cried for 15 minutes	

Day 2	11.30 a.m.	cried for 5 minutes	
	2.30 p.m.	cried for 15 minutes	2 occasions

Day 3	Looked like crying but did not	0

Day 4	No crying	0

Day 5	No crying	0

He could have also shown these results this way:

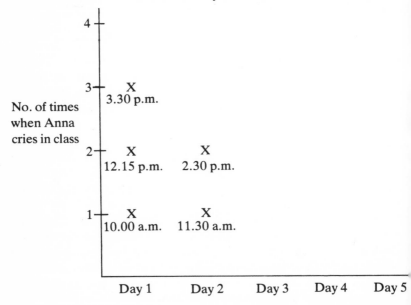

No. of times when Anna cries in class	Mon	Tue	Wed	Thur	Fri
3	Cried at 3.30 p.m.				
2	Cried at 12.15 p.m.	Cried at 2.30 p.m.			
1	Cried at 10.00 a.m.	Cried at 11.30 a.m.	0	0	0

Days of the week

or even like this. This is the easiest way to record someone's behaviour.

No. of times when Anna cries in class

	Day 1	Day 2	Day 3	Day 4	Day 5
4					
3	X 3.30 p.m.				
2	X 12.15 p.m.	X 2.30 p.m.			
1	X 10.00 a.m.	X 11.30 a.m.			

Carefully check consequences

Everybody knows that what happens after a behaviour will have a considerable influence on whether the behaviour is repeated. Why do mothers smack their children when caught with their fingers in the biscuit tin? In the hope that the child will think twice before finishing the chocolate biscuits again. Why do many men invest their money in flowers, and chocolates and good dinners for new girlfriends? They have learnt that most women feel quite happy about seeing them again if a bit pampered the first time round. But as we have tried to show, making the consequences of a behaviour extremely nice or devastatingly nasty will not necessarily affect the behaviour. The antecedents or background may be playing a major part in the continuation of the problem.

But the consequences of a behaviour do have a major role to play. In Anna's case, her behaviour after the new programme began was called classic for a good reason. If a behaviour is being maintained by consequences – as her crying was – it often increases in frequency sharply when the expected consequences do not occur. On the first day when Ian was not making the consequences of crying pleasant as he had been doing previously, Anna had three tearful outbursts quite close together in time. This was more than in the previous week. There is a good reason why this increase of unwanted behaviour happens.

Supposing every time a three-year-old cries in public, his mother quietens him with chocolate or by instantly giving into his demands. She is *reinforcing* his bad behaviour, literally teaching him that by yelling and being naughty he can make pleasant things happen. Before long, mothers get irritated by this type of crying behaviour and decide to stop giving in to their children. Immediately the tantrums become worse in the same way as Anna stepped up her tearful outbursts. Tantrums will grow in ferocity and frequency because the child has learned in the past that a good loud yell at the checkout desk will earn a sweetie from the rack. When the reinforcement does not come, he will yell louder. His mother may smack him, threaten him, but the tantrum will get worse until he has his way.

The only way to change the behaviour is to stop reinforcing it by rewarding it with sweets or acquiescence. It takes steel nerves for a mother to decide not to give in and to brave the stares of other mothers, the sometimes disapproving looks of a checkout girl, as her child screams and yells. If you embark on such a course of action, beware, for on several consecutive shopping days the child may continue to kick up a fuss until eventually he learns that no screaming, no tantrum behaviour will be reinforced. Once he has learned that lesson, the behaviour will stop completely.

It took Anna only a short while to learn that her crying behaviour no longer brought pleasant consequences. This happened quickly because Ian, her teacher, stuck rigidly to his strategy. Returning to the mother at the checkout, if she gives in just once she will be right back at the beginning. Her son will have discovered anew, that by making a sufficient nuisance of himself he can get his own way.

When something pleasant happens to a person after he has behaved in a certain way it is more likely that he will behave in that way again. The person has been *reinforced* for his behaviour. Psychologists use the term *reinforcement* to describe any consequent event which is likely to make the behaviour occur in future.

People find different things reinforcing. Some reinforcements, like a child being given a chocolate as a reward for good behaviour, are almost universal in their appeal. Others are more obscure. We know of one child who will repeat practically anything if reinforced by his father's swinging him by his ankles.

Just in the case of Anna, it is a common fault among teachers or parents to reinforce unwittingly behaviours which have become a problem. Often the way in which a parent or teacher attempts to punish a child may in reality be reinforcing the unwanted behaviour.

Sometimes teachers will move a naughty, difficult child to the front of the class and have him sit by them. The teacher's intention is to keep the child quiet. That aim is often only partly achieved. The child is quiet while the teacher sits at the desk but when she moves away, he begins to be a nuisance. If the teacher regularly calls the child to her side after bad behaviour, the child will quickly learn that behaving badly brings the rewards of more teacher attention.

When focusing on the consequences of a problem behaviour, look carefully. Ask yourself the question, "Is there any way that these consequences are reinforcing the behaviour?" "Is the person being reinforced by the results of his or her behaviour?"

The power of reinforcement
If the consequences of a behaviour are highly reinforcing it is possible the balance between antecedent, background and consequences is top heavy. The behaviour will be repeated frequently almost irrespective of antecedents or background. A powerful example of this is the

behaviour of teenagers involved in their first romance. They find seeing their girlfriend or boyfriend is more reinforcing than completing homework assignments, returning home early in the evening, or babysitting. Teachers and parents who try to change their behaviour back to 'studious, stay at homes' discover they fail unless they build in the desired reinforcement – fitting the boyfriend or girlfriend somewhere into the scenario. Keeping their son or daughter in, working upstairs, may lead to the often reported behaviour of shinning down the drainpipe in search of a more reinforcing situation. Parental anger before or after the event all becomes irrelevant. Consequences rule, O.K!

What people find reinforcing varies. Looking at consequences of behaviour it is possible to be duped into thinking the situation is not pleasant for the person when it is actually highly reinforcing.

Jonathan was an eight-year-old who stole all his brother's sweets and chocolates. As a punishment he was ticked off by his parents and forced to eat sweets for breakfast, lunch and supper the next day. His parents predicted that he would get sick of sweets and regret not being allowed to eat good food. In fact, their strategy had no effect on his behaviour and he stepped up his stealing. Although it looked like the consequences were punishing, Jonathan enjoyed the sweets and probably also liked being made special at mealtimes. Needless to say, his mother did not give him enough sweets to make him sick which would have been unpleasant.

Even when his mother tried to make the consequences more unpleasant by giving the family all his favourite foods while he was on his sweet diet, this only served to restate his special situation.

Reinforcers are powerful in another way too. Not only does a reinforcer have the power to make behaviour occur *again*, but the *frequency* with which a person received a reinforcement also has an effect on behaviour.

Supposing a boy cleans the family car every weekend and is paid thirty pence. The boy living next door also cleans his family's car once a week. Sometimes his father thanks him and tells him how pleased he is and sometimes he gives him money for the cinema or to go to a football match. The second boy never knows for sure whether he will be rewarded by more than praise. Which boy will be most willing to continue cleaning the car.

It will be the second boy. The first is always paid. He can predict he will receive his thirty pence. There is no uncertainty. Psychologists call this situation a 'constant reinforcement schedule', i.e. he always receives the same reinforcement after the behaviour.

The second boy never knows whether he will be reinforced or not. He cannot predict what the reinforcement will be or indeed if he will receive any at all. But he can predict that if he is reinforced it will be extremely pleasurable. He might clean the car five times in a row for nothing and be rewarded the sixth time by a day at the motor scramble. On the seventh occasion, his father might give him a pound and on the eighth nothing except a thank you. He is on what psychologists call 'an intermittent reinforcement schedule', i.e. he is reinforced occasionally.

There are many examples of people successfully working intermittent reinforcement schedules in everyday life. Many girls operate such systems brilliantly by refusing to go out with their boyfriends on enough occasions to keep their man in a lather of enthusiasm. If they saw their boyfriends every day they might well become tired of the experience before becoming dependent!

Behaviours which are learned through an intermittent reinforcement schedule are harder to unlearn than those acquired via constant reinforcement. People go on performing the same action time and again in the hope of reinforcement because they did not always receive it before. Those who are constantly reinforced swiftly learn that no reinforcement for behaviours are forthcoming and they stop.

It is because of this well recognised fact that consistency of handling is so important when trying to change behaviour. That is also why observing the complained of behaviour closely *before* deciding what to do about it is so vital.

If a behaviour is seen to be occurring because the consequences of the behaviour are of a reinforcing nature, just one relaxation, one inconsistency in the pattern designed for change is enough to cause that behaviour to continue longer. The teacher in the case of Anna achieved swift results because having been forwarned to expect an increase in both frequency and strength of the crying outburst he was consistent in all his reactions. The actions he took were executed in a gentle kindly manner but firmly so that Anna could not interpret what happened as a punishment or unkindness. She was given the time she needed to talk at the teacher's convenience and not on demand thus transferring control of the situation from the pupil to teacher.

It is important to be consistent when you want to help someone to unlearn an undesirable behaviour.

Revision
1 A behaviour is maintained by the balance between A, B and C events. It is not easy to see this balance.
2 Objective observation is of paramount importance. Selective observation is essential. Learn to observe:
  a the behaviour
  b the background
  c the antecedents
  d the consequences
  e the effects of the consequences.
3 Reinforcement is a technical word. Psychologists use this to describe a consequent event which makes the behaviour more likely to be repeated.
4 A constant reinforcement schedule is one where the behaviour is reinforced on every possible occasion. An intermittent reinforcement schedule refers to the situation where the behaviour is only occasionally reinforced.
5 Behaviours which have in the past been taught by reinforcing occasionally (intermittently reinforced behaviours) are more difficult to unlearn than behaviours which have been taught by reinforcing the person every time he behaved that way (constantly reinforced behaviour).
6 Plan a strategy and stick to it like glue or until your records show clearly that it is not working.

7

Unlearning old behaviour
Techniques for managing disruptive behaviours

Recorded observations offer a key to changing behaviour. Not a key like a house key with which you open the door and light floods in, but a key for cracking a code.

The behaviour you wish to change may be governed by antecedents, background, or consequences. Observations enable people to perceive behaviour more clearly, almost like a film director. Through interpreting observations objectively a person can assess any situation before planning for change through rearranging the events which surround behaviour problems.

It is a common experience to realise that to change someone else's behaviour, a parent or teacher first has to change something about their own habitual behaviour.

Good observation makes people become more objective and aware of how their behaviour as well as others are all part of a whole, like a big jigsaw puzzle. Once the total situation is understood it is relatively easy to decide which bits of the puzzle need adjusting in order to influence the unwanted behaviours. Almost always it is the adult whose behaviour is the first to be changed. He is in control of his actions and able to change in a way a child or adolescent cannot.

In choosing which bits of the ABC puzzle to juggle around, almost certainly he will concentrate more on antecedent, or the consequent events or will decide to change the background. He will not be trying to change all three at once. He may decide to focus on one aspect like antecedents but may also have to make minor changes to the background or consequences to get the balance of the picture right.

There are many different strategies for rearranging the puzzle. Some can be used in almost any situation, others have very specific applications. In describing some of the strategies which we use often, recommend to others and find effective, we have split them into four groupings. Obviously the first three of these relate to changing antecedents, background and consequences. The fourth is an idea which we have not mentioned yet – teaching a competing behaviour.

The first possibility we explore when facing an unwanted behaviour is the possibility of teaching a competing behaviour. If there is none available, then there are various approaches specifically appropriate for altering A, B or C events.

Teaching competing behaviours
It is satisfying to help someone to unlearn an unwanted behaviour by teaching them a new skill which prevents the unwanted behaviour occurring. Every new skill or behaviour a person learns makes their repertoire of behaviours wider. There are more things they can do and thus they have more choices in any situation.

In institutions for handicapped people bad habits of an extreme nature like rocking or head banging are sometimes seen. At one time a walk through a ward of handicapped adolescents might be punctuated by boys sitting in a hunched position rocking back and forth rhythmically. They rocked as if in time to an unseen metronome with eyes staring vacantly straight ahead. Others could be seen wearing protective helmets and thumping their heads against walls or floorboards. Often such wards had no books, games, toys or even posters on the walls. There were few nurses, and their time was taken up by physical caring only. Feeding, making beds and toiletting left little time to spend with patients in other activities. By reorganising nursing time staff were able to begin teaching competing behaviours and these undesirable patient activities were reduced. How can a boy rock rhythmically if he is sitting on a chair at a table completing a puzzle? Who can bang his head when out for a walk, or engaged in some other activity which is taking up his entire attention?

An example of teaching a competing behaviour in the home is, for instance, the mother who teaches her young child to make her a cup of tea under supervision rather than playing with the electric kettle indiscriminantly. One mother who found her small daughter feeding the baby glass marbles taught her to feed him with his bottle instead. It is no accident that people who are trying to give up smoking fiddle with 'worry beads' or indulge in other types of competing behaviours which make it difficult to smoke during the first tough days. Perhaps you could think of two competing behaviours to cope with the following:

1 Pushing over smaller children.
2 Scribbling over the wallpaper with a felt tip pen.

1 Successful strategies to stop pushing:
   a Teach the child to help smaller children who have fallen down.
   b Encourage the child to play with smaller children in situations where adults are in control.
     E.g. puppet theatre, train set.
   c Push or pull a younger child around on a toy car.

2 Scribbling over wallpaper:
   a Teach the child to use alternative surfaces like dot-to-dot pictures.
   b Write on a blackboard with chalk.
   c Using finger paints in the kitchen.
   Always keep felt tips in a special box in the living room.

Teaching one or more competing behaviours is probably *the* most effective way of dealing with undesirable behaviour!

Strategies for rearranging antecedents
A daily showdown occurs in many households when a parent utters one immortal line "O.K. it's time for bed!" Until adolescents reach sixteen or so when most are allowed to decide their own bed times, the announcement is liable to be met with doleful expressions at best or a full-scale force nine row at the worst. There are ways of avoiding such a confrontation.

Good news for bad
The situation can be transformed by lessening the bad news or turning it into good. Just substitute a signal for a happy event! The announce-ment, "It's bath time and Dad's in charge", in some households produces a stampede to the bathroom with Mum stepping smartly aside to avoid being trampled. The statement, "As soon as everyone's in bed Mum will bring a hot chocolate", or the promise that Dad will come and read a story (preferably a book which is stopped each night

at a cliff hanger) can have the effect of bedtime becoming a 'looked forward to' time. In each case something slightly unpleasant is hidden by something obviously good.

Early warning

Using 'Early Warning Systems' to prevent antecedents having unpleasant affects are equally helpful. If you warn a person something is going to happen shortly before the event, it lessens the impact of the bad news. Some parents overcome the bedtime problem by warning their children twenty minutes beforehand. With young children taking them to the kitchen clock and going through the time hallowed ritual of, "When the big hand gets to the six it will be time for bed" makes bedtime less threatening and getting there more fun. Children discover that telling the time even to this extent is reinforcing.

Another way is to help the child set a household timer for the time interval. Parents frequently report that their children remind them when there are only a few minutes left to bedtime or that the timer has emitted its pre-ringing tone. In most instances parents say their children go to bed without fussing.

These early warnings are successful because they prepare children for clearing up, for stopping watching television, for coming in from the garden or in other words changing a pleasant activity for a slightly unpleasant one. The child may dread the end of the twenty minutes when he must leave his toys or trains. It is less of a wrench than someone walking in and saying, "Right, bedtime" when the child is in the middle of moving a goods train into a siding!

Give clear instructions

Sometimes bedtime is a problem because children are not clear exactly what they should do when told "Right, off to bed then!" 'Going to bed' can involve a child in many activities including going upstairs, bathing, having a hot drink, washing teeth, reading in bed, and finally putting out the light and trying to sleep. Wise parents ensure that a bedtime ritual is taught where children are clear about the order of events and exactly what tasks they or their parents are expected to perform within this ritual. Clear instructions equal clear performances!

Clever teachers can deal effectively with problems like dinner queue jumping, stampedes between classrooms, or jostling cloakroom scenes. Such teachers make sure that the children know exactly what is expected of them and sometimes rehearse these activities with the children from time to time. This means that children are not only told what to do but given ample opportunities to practise.

Clear instructions can often change antecedent events so much that no other interventions are necessary – the behaviour changes!

Your turn now!

Just as bedtime is a source of aggravation for children, punctuality causes many arguments between adults. It is remarkable how many men who are never late have wives who are hopelessly unable to be on time (or vice versa). Early warning combined with appropriate reinforcement for better time keeping can have a startlingly beneficial effect on punctuality.

Use a system of exchanging good news for bad or an early warning or clear instructions to deal with the following problems:

Problem 1   The husband who stays in the potting shed for up to twenty minutes after his wife has told him Sunday lunch is on the table.

Problem 2   The wife who spends ages 'getting ready' to go out while her husband stamps around downstairs watching the clock.

Strategies for changing the background

The period of observation may show that unwanted behaviour occurs exclusively in one place. It might be demonstrated that this behaviour occurs more in one setting than another, or that certain conditions are always present in the background.

In any of these cases, there are ways of changing the background.

Removing temptation

One of our clients reported that her small daughter was beginning to throw tantrums. More often than not these occurred on shopping trips to one of the two self-service stores in her village. Close investigation showed that the tantrum began as they approached the checkout and centred on whether or not the child would have a sweet.

This mother decided that the simplest way to stop the tantrums was to remove the temptation. On her next shopping trip she studiously avoided noticing when her daughter took a bar of chocolate and ignored her as she solemnly tore off the wrapper and took a large bite out of the end. The checkout girl finished totting up her shopping and the mother paid her bill. The girl noticed the child munching happily and realised the chocolate had not been paid for and asked for money. "Oh dear", said the mother, "I'd better see the store manager."

The mother took her daughter and the soggy chocolate to the manager. She smiled a charming bland greeting and said, "My child took this off the shelf while the checkout girl and I were busy. I do think it is such a silly place to put sweets. Infants do not understand they are for sale. You must lose a fortune this way!"

The startled store manager stared at the messy chocolate in his hand but before he could speak she smiled and left the shop cordially waving goodbye! The next time she went into the store, there were no sweets, chocolates or other temptations at the checkout counter. There was no tantrum from her daughter either!

Although this is one extreme way of removing temptation, the principle is always the same. Anticipate what circumstances allow a problem behaviour to occur and remove these.

One little girl used to wake up early each morning. While her parents slept, she would creep downstairs and open cupboard doors, tipping their contents all over the floor. As she was only three it was difficult to explain just why this behaviour was such a problem. So the parents solved this difficulty by putting child proof bolts on the doors of the cupboards. Just as important, they taught her the competing behaviour of playing quietly in her bedroom each morning when she woke up.

The most obvious example of 'removing temptation' is the smoker who begins his New Year resolution to stop smoking by ceremoniously shredding and throwing his store of cigarettes into the dustbin.

Change the setting

Preventing problems by making sure the elements conducive to un- wanted behaviour are not present is a neat way of bringing behaviour under control. The adult takes positive action to prevent the child from being given the opportunity to misbehave. In classrooms it might mean separating two children or placing one under the teacher's eye. Alter- natively the teacher might examine the work the child is given to see whether the level of difficulty is right and the subject matter is interesting. There are few things more likely to contribute to children behaving badly in class than badly explained instructions, ill conceived lesson plans or work being too hard or too simple. A wise teacher looks at her behaviour and the elements of background setting she controls before saying a child is a problem because of *his* faults. It is a sensible

parent who applies the same rule before falling for the easy way out: "He's just like his dad/uncle/mum/grandfather."

Introduce a prompt
Sometimes observation shows that the background is contributing to unwanted behaviour, but it is difficult to remove temptation or change the setting. For instance when you take your children to have tea with an elderly friend, especially if your friend is not used to having young children around, trouble seems inevitable. To avoid such occasions becoming ones where children misbehave and tempers flare, some parents introduce a simple system of prompts. To do this successfully, the children are told rules of behaviour are expected.

The children and parents agree a code word or gesture which will be used when they are behaving properly.

Secret prompts are both effective and amusing. One teacher we know used them to control the level of noise in his lab. He had two cards, one black and one white in his pocket. He would hold up one of these as he walked around the class checking work or helping groups of children with their task assignment. Black meant "too much noise!" while white said "noise level just fine". His classroom management was the most effective in the entire school and he rarely had to raise his voice!

You try it!
How would you change the behaviour of a child who snatches back one of his toys from a visitor with the cry, "S'mine!" Would you remove temptation, change the scene or perhaps use a secret prompt?

Strategies for changing consequences
Whenever consequences have a major effect on behaviour almost always the adult has to change his behaviour. Changing consequences is frequently used to deal with behaviours which happen too often. Some of the strategies employed are:

Attention
The most powerful tool available to any adult trying to control a child's behaviour (and in some instances, another adult's) is attention. By attention we mean looking at, talking to, being in direct contact with another person and making it clear to that person that they are, for the time being, the focal point of interest. The trick is to use attention selectively.

In a child's world, adults are all important. Adults have the power to make nice things happen like going on a helter skelter or buying an ice cream. Adults also have the power to punish. To a five-year-old, an adult of over five foot six is a veritable giant. Large adults tower over small children. Certainly adults control the world the child lives in. Children have a natural desire for adult attention, "Look Mummy, I've made a sand castle". "Daddy, I got all my sums right". "Read me a story". All of these are blatant attempts to receive reinforcement. "Isn't that a lovely sand castle, who's a clever fellow?", "All your sums? Well done!" "Come, bring me the book and you can sit on my lap".

A considerable amount of problem behaviour relates to children trying to gain attention inappropriately. A typical situation might be when a mother has a friend in for coffee. On several occasions the child tries to get her mother's attention and is told, "Go away, I'll come and look later, I'm talking to Aunty Jean". Eventually the child knocks the flowers over and is covered with water, or begins to cry or in some other way by naughty behaviour, forces her mother to pay attention to her and not to the lady sipping coffee. Attention is to a child as sunshine is to a flower.

It is through other people's attention that we receive information concerning our behaviour. When people talk they often maintain eye contact. The conversation continues because the person speaking can see reflected in the listener's face a range of reactions. The listener, by listening in a manner which the speaker can see is attentive, maintains the speaker's behaviour. If a listener looks away, stares out of the window, turns their back or in other obvious ways indicates inattention, the speaker's voice will falter and gradually cease altogether if the attention is totally removed.

An obvious example of the effect of attention on a speaker can be seen from behaviour in clubs or theatres. Occasionally young comedians are given opportunities to perform before the main act. Even to a casual observer the situation is excruciatingly difficult for the comedian. He begins his act. The audience waits to be amused. The jokes are poor and after a few minutes of polite listening the audience's attention shifts to more interesting discussions at their table, or a rush of drinks orders before the main act. The comedian desperately tells more jokes and gradually his voice is drowned by his audience. Few can remain on stage for long without the attention of an audience.

Good manipulators of their own behaviour can switch attention on and off with the same ease as turning on an electric light! There are degrees of attention. A teacher can demonstrate approval to a child by as small an action as catching his eye across the class and giving a light approving wink. He could give a beaming smile. He might smile and call across the room, "That's nice, Bill, you seem to be getting on well this morning". If he wanted to reinforce the child more he could go to his side, look at his work, talk about the good aspects and maybe touch him on his shoulder before moving away. The penultimate accolade in a class could be to stop the class working and call everyone's attention to what a well behaved, hard working person a child is and how good his work has been that day. The ultimate might be to send the child to the headteacher with his work for compliments from the secretary and the Head. Attention used as a reinforcer is economic of time and likely to make desirable behaviours occur repeatedly. Praising and commenting on good behaviour increases the number of pleasant encounters which occur in a classroom, the room becomes a happier place to be in, and teachers become perceived as human beings rather than ogres. Successful teachers know the golden rule is: *Never Use a Bigger Reinforcer than Necessary.*

The secret of using selective attention to control behaviour is to turn on attention only when the child is doing what you want and to switch off when he is not. Obviously there are behaviours which it is impossible to ignore, but if the undesired habit is not disruptive, nor interfering with others, then it can be safely ignored.

Learning to ignore behaviour is acquiring an art which many people find difficult. One habit which irritates teachers in class, or parents at home, is the child who walks up while an adult is talking to someone and deliberately interrupts the conversation. One way of ignoring the child's behaviour is to continue talking. The child may position himself so that not only is he pulling the adult's sleeve, but also trying to establish eye contact. The most effective way of ignoring this behaviour is to turn your back so that the child cannot interrupt and to keep showing the child the back of your head while maintaining an animated conversation to its conclusion. Then and only then the child is given attention.

To 'ignore' in this context means to *cease to recognise the existence* of the offender. He can see from the adult's body language, lack of eye contact and refusal to respond that as far as these adults are concerned 'he is not there'.

Thus if a teacher decides to ignore a child when he wanders around the classroom, and to reinforce him with attention when he is in his seat

Never use a bigger reinforcer than necessary

though not necessarily working, the teacher must act as though she literally does not see the child when out of seat. If the teacher allows her eyes to follow the child around the room, even that degree of attention can have the effect of maintaining the behaviour. The child perceives he is being watched and will predictably maintain his behaviour. He will be anticipating teacher attention even if this is only in the form of a reprimand. The teacher must selectively use attention with great precision to gain the desired results – the child staying in seat. At the beginning the child needs to be reinforced in short regular intervals for being in seat and then the intervals lengthened. The ignoring occurs only when he is out of seat and the attention when he is in. When using selective attention, it is sensible to place the child on a *constant reinforcement schedule* to begin with, reducing to an *intermittent schedule* and finally holding the child's behaviour at the required level through a *maintenance schedule* which would consist of the lowest possible level of reinforcement.

Natasha was a three-year-old who did not know how to smile. When she was pleased where anyone else would have smiled she pulled a face, grimaced and contorted her features into a rude expression. She attended a day nursery for children from problem homes. Her mother and father were divorcing. The mother was a dour woman who never smiled and rarely changed her blank, sour, unpleasant expression. The matron of the nursery observed Natasha during a week. She concluded that this child had never been taught how or when to smile. Observing the mother's face, anyone could guess how this situation had occurred.

The staff set up a mirror in the corner of the nursery and surrounded it with pictures of happy faces on the left and sad faces on the right. They made two hand puppets, one showing a smile, the other a frown. Daily for a few minutes at a time she and a member of the staff played what became known as the 'Happy, Sad Game'. Natasha chose a puppet and was encouraged to imitate the puppet's expression. Slowly the adult playing with her taught her how to smile.

Gradually by paying attention to her smiles and not to her grimaces Natasha learnt the difference between the expressions. Throughout the rest of the day, the staff paid extra attention to her when she appeared to be trying to smile. They ignored her grimaces completely. After six weeks, Natasha was smiling like everyone else.

Smiling programmes may seem a little odd but there are many boys and girls who for a variety of reasons wander around with morose, glum expressions. In one junior school there was a boy who by his air of permanent misery was irritating the staff and not making any friends. People avoided him. This caused problems in lessons where the children were told to pair off for a special activity. At the school sports he never got a chance to run a three-legged race.

He was being discussed in the staff room one day while the school psychologist was there for coffee at breaktime. Almost as a joke the psychologist suggested putting the boy on a popularity programme. Before many moments had passed, the discussion had turned into a serious debate on how the staff could change the boy's behaviour. All the staff agreed to smile at the boy and, or, speak to him every day at least once. There were eleven members of staff. His class teacher volunteered to find three pleasant things to say to him every day. To begin with the teacher thought he might even have to contrive this by giving the child an easy task and complimenting him on its inevitable completion. Someone suggested a method of recording to make sure each staff member did their bit daily. A chart was pinned up on the staff notice board.

Someone else recommended that if there was anything about the boy which could be remarked on, like new socks or clean hair, it was important to do so. All agreed these new, kind remarks should be seen and heard by as many children as possible. This plan was devised in a spirit of fun but with serious intent because everyone agreed it must have been hell to be as unpopular as this child. There were several doubts expressed whether staff could act well enough at the beginning to be convincing.

This 'smiling programme' as it became known was not instantly successful. It was several weeks before the boy obviously changed. He began to smile back, he began to nervously produce tiny remarks in response to the staff and after a term he no longer stood out like a sore thumb in class. He never became popular but he managed to be accepted and to have a few friends who called on him in the evening. In fact he became unexceptional.

It was all due to selective attention. The school staff were reinforcing the behaviours they wanted to see more of, so these behaviours increased. As these were the kinds of behaviours which made for 'popularity', so he became more popular.

Pupil attention selectively controlled can be used to change behaviour. Ruth was a girl who was often seen raising her hand, asking 'silly questions', calling out in lessons or walking up to the teacher at awkward moments. She annoyed her teacher by refusing to answer questions, but would take up a good deal of teacher time, chatting about just every topic except her schoolwork or the task set. Her teacher claimed that Ruth was 'seriously maladjusted'.

The school psychologist suggested to the teacher that Ruth should be seated next to Sean who was a quiet, hard-working boy who had few friends in the class. Ruth and Sean were asked to report on each other's 'on task' behaviour after certain lessons. They were also shown how to record in a book when the other had been working well. Four or five weeks later, a delighted teacher reported that this strategy had been a huge success. Ruth was in her seat and working for most of the day and she and Sean had become almost inseparable friends.[6]

Reinforce good behaviour

Teachers single out children when they are being naughty and tell them to stop in the hope that they will. They possibly do for a few minutes and then are likely to start misbehaving again, only to be told off again, and the cycle repeated. All psychologists are familiar with research findings concerning children who are often out of seat in class. The cycle in this case is: Johnny gets up, wanders around class, teacher says "Go and sit down". Johnny sits down. Ten minutes later the teacher sees him at the other side of the classroom once more. She tells him to sit down and so on.

In a typical example one teacher was observed for a two-week period. During the period of observation it was recorded that he was spending 70 per cent of his time admonishing children for being out of seat, not working, fooling around or talking. The remaining 30 per cent of his time was spent teaching. He was then asked to ignore disruptive behaviours and told not to comment on these. At the same time he was told to congratulate his pupils deliberately when they were doing the things he asked. He was also asked to hold up good behaviour as an example of what he wanted from his pupils.

The study shows an immediate upsurge of bad behaviour when he began invoking the new methods. After a few days, the general behaviour in class began to improve. Two weeks later a further period of observation showed he was spending 40 per cent of his time on behaviour control and 60 per cent in active teaching. The earlier situation had almost been reversed.

Research studies repeatedly show how much more effective it is to note the positive than to pick out bad behaviour for punishment. Paradoxically this is opposite to the manner in which most people behave when they try to control others.

It is not surprising comedians laugh at the carping mother in law, the nagging wife, the chauvinistic husband and the pernickety boss. These characters are known to everyone as stereotypes of people who try to change others by being particularly nasty.

Changing bad behaviours for good ought to happen in a happy positive way. Someone's behaviour might need changing because they are 'monsters' and causing other people trouble, but the end result

---

[6] This case history is reported in: Hedderly, R. (1978) 'Orange Juice Theory' *Journal of the Association of Educational Psychologists.* Vol. 4, No. 9. Pages 24–28.

should be aimed at making everybody concerned cope better with life and have fewer bad experiences. Thus all plans for change should be laid with an accent on the positive not the negative aspects of behaviour.

Sharing responsibility
Parents complain to us frequently about teenagers who refuse to help with daily chores. The list of chores is always growing but old favourites include tidying bedrooms, washing up, taking the dog out, putting bicycles away properly, doing homework early in the evening, cleaning out rabbit hutches, helping with shopping, cooking the evening meal or babysitting and house cleaning. It is understandable these things become focuses for argument. Chores are not fun. There are many adults, let alone children, who would be delighted to get out of the necessary hard work of keeping a house clean and tidy, a garden neat and the car washed. One way of turning these chores into something better is to tune them into a reward system. Some parents make the reward something which is inevitable anyway but can be speeded up to suit the circumstances. The aim is to make the control of future events a shared responsibility between parent and child.

Denise was a thirteen-year-old who refused to do any work whatsoever. She had a younger brother with a physical handicap and he demanded a lot of time and attention from their parents. She refused to help, saying things like "Why should I? You're always so busy with Peter you never do anything for me!"

She needed a new winter coat for school. Her mother took her to a local shop and allowed her to pick out the coat she wanted. The coat was paid for and the manageress was asked to keep it in the shop until required. Back home, Denise and mother made a wall chart. The chart was divided into days on the vertical axis and showed a number of household chores on the horizontal axis. Denise could earn a set number of points for each task she completed. Activities she disliked most carried the highest number of points and those she liked, which were few, but included doing the ironing, were rated low. If Denise earned 50 per cent of the points available daily she would be able to reach the target and pick up her coat in exactly four weeks, the length of time her clever mother had worked out would bring them into the cold weather when she really would need the coat! If she did everything she would receive the coat in two weeks. Denise earned her coat in under four weeks!

This system had an advantage. Her mother was forced to notice everything Denise did at least once a day when the points were put on the chart. This led to more "thank you's", more complimentary statements and Denise beginning to see herself as a valued person in the family because she was repeatedly being told positive things. Her mother never chided her for the chores she did not do, only reinforced her for doing good.

Sharing responsibility is a good way of coping with many problems, especially those which crop up across a generation gap.

Time Out

Time Out is a technique used by psychologists to control behaviour. It gives teachers and parents a planned approach to child management but if wrongly used can become punishing.

There are times when people cannot behave appropriately. They become excited or irrational and are unable immediately to change their behaviour on request. When a child is stopped from fighting or has done something wrong and bursts into near hysterical tears, or is stubbornly refusing to tell the truth and blustering desperately, he is not able to examine his behaviour calmly or even listen to what people are saying. Take a child away from these kinds of tricky situations and leave him on his own in a quiet area for not longer than ten minutes. This gives him Time Out from the bad experience. Time Out means time away from a situation. Later when the child is calm it is possible to talk quietly about the misbehaviour. An adult can suggest ways of behaving better in the future in an atmosphere in which the child can listen, accept corrections and work out a method of apology.

When children reach heights of disagreeableness, some parents say, "Right, go to your room and stay there". This is not a carefully planned Time Out management scheme. It is a punishment. Apart from only buying temporary peace and quiet it is not effective at changing behaviour in the long term either.

What happens when a child is on his own is fairly predictable. For the first few minutes, he cries, kicks things, screams or just sits and seethes with anger. None of these activities last long when people are on their own unless reinforced by parents or others paying attention. Hence after a few minutes he begins to calm down and may begin to think about what happened. After this his thoughts may wander to the book he is reading each night in bed, or his model aeroplane half finished on his desk, or he might decide to discover what is under the corner of the torn wallpaper and begin systematically stripping the wall. Within fifteen minutes most children have forgotten why they are on their own and have become engrossed in other activities. Half an hour later many children are beginning to be resentful at being in their room and seeing Mum and Dad as bullies, and the good which could have come out of the separation from the family is gone.

If a parent leaves the child alone until there is silence upstairs or about ten minutes have elapsed, the experience can be positive and called Time Out. Such controlled separation gives the parent an opportunity to calm down too. He or she is able to go to the child, discuss the problem calmly and bring the child back to the family group. Time Out used properly is effective and positive.

If a parent decides to use Time Out as an intervention for change, it is recommended that the periods of Time Out are recorded, together with the precise reason why the child was put on Time Out and the aftermath thirty minutes later. It has been known for Time Out to be ineffective or for the technique to develop into nothing more than a punishment. Recording makes it possible to judge whether it is producing a change and also for the parent to keep an eye on the length of time involved.

Schools where Time Out is used in a positive manner report children reach a point where they voluntarily place themselves on Time Out. There are many anecdotes about children finding a classroom or playground incident escalating past their control and requesting permission to use Time Out.

One case where Time Out turned out to be almost a magic wand treatment concerned a small boy who was at a Special School. Alan had his own brand of temper tantrums and on occasion caused physical harm not only to adults and children but to inanimate objects like large plate glass windows.

The parent and teacher began recording the incidents of tantrums which they claimed occurred as often as four or five times each day. After two weeks the evidence forced them to revise this opinion to a truer estimate of between four and five a week.

The school holidays were starting and the mother elected to try Time Out. In her house there was a small cloakroom by the front door which contained nothing more than a lavatory and wash basin. She chose this as the Time Out area and laboriously explained to Alan what would happen if he threw a tantrum and checked out he understood.

A couple of days later he misbehaved and she placed him in the cloakroom. She hovered out of sight leaving the door open in case he

decided to run out or begin to wreck the room. He screamed for a while, quietened down and after a few minutes of silence she allowed him to go on playing as if no upset had occurred. Alan accepted her strategy and when necessary (three times in the first week) he was placed on Time Out. Over the six weeks of the holiday his tantrum behaviour was successfully extinguished. Alan even responded positively to the warning of Time Out when he began to display pre-tantrum behaviour in other areas like the town centre or the swimming baths.

This using of Time Out in public places has caused one or two psychologists extreme embarrassment. One psychologist had a group of children in an empty amusement park. A boy misbehaved. He was told to remain by some railings on Time Out for five minutes. A couple of minutes later a family group appeared and the boy, who up till then had been silent, collapsed into hysterical tears. Predictably the mother moved over to comfort him. The boy told her at the top of his voice how cruel and unkind that big bully of a psychologist was and somehow failed to mention how two minutes before he had wrapped the chains of a swing around another boy's neck!

Physical restraint
Sometimes when children lose control and become flailing bundles of arms and legs, dangerous to other children and themselves, an immediate method of reducing the risk of harm becomes essential. Hitting the child in such circumstances may increase his aggressive behaviour. Catching him in a half-nelson may be briefly effective but is painful and a child might claim afterwards that he had been bullied. Thus if physical restraint is used in a classroom or at home it is best used in a manner which stops the child's activity but neither frightens nor hurts.

The best way to restrain a child if this becomes necessary is by holding him at the top of the arms above the elbows with an equal pressure on each arm. This can become a bear hug or remain as hands exerting sufficient control over the upper arm muscle to stop the child hitting or kicking. To avoid being kicked it is better to approach from behind but as it is frightening to be held by someone in a vice-like grip from behind, the sooner the child can be swung to face the holder the better. While holding, the adult should repeat like a Hindu mantra, a formula such as "You are upset now, soon you will start feeling less angry and as soon as you are feeling better, I will not hold you tightly". Obviously the physical size of adult and child bears a relationship as to how successfully physical restraint can be applied. There was a wee Scots girl of five foot two teaching a group of difficult adolescent boys who found she could restrain even the largest. When upset many people are looking for help and accept even minimal restraint as a way out of tricky moments.

Like Time Out there is a danger that physical restraint can become unnecessarily punishing. Restraint should always be accompanied with kindness and followed as soon as the child is calm by a discussion about the incident. Children should also be given clear advice on how they could have behaved and a better strategy to employ in a situation next time.

Most effective of all, people can be taught how to restrain themselves. This technique was employed successfully with a twelve-year-old boy. He was given a tape recorder and the instruction that when he was angry, he was to go to a quiet place and record exactly what he thought and how he felt. The tapes were never listened to by anyone but himself, yet this was sufficient to enable him to remain calm.

Selecting your strategy

Before deciding on a strategy or a technique to employ and a programme of intervention to cause a change, analyse when, how, where and how often the behaviour occurs. This use of an ABC approach can only follow selective observation. The intervention you choose will probably carry within it one or more of the methods discussed in this chapter; selective use of attention, teaching competing behaviours, adding interest to activities, rewarding desired behaviours and removing temptations, turning good from bad, warning well in advance or using Time Out and maybe even physical restraint. Whichever strategy is adopted, whatever plan you make, it will be more successful if it is founded on a positive approach. Behaviour always changes given a positive nudge or a friendly push in the right direction!

Remember:
1 The first way of dealing with unwanted behaviour is to consider teaching a competing skill which makes it difficult for the person to misbehave.
2 Three ways of changing *antecedent* events which may prevent the behaviour from occurring are:
   a Exchanging good news for bad.
   b Giving an early warning.
   c Giving clear instructions.

Always reinforce good behaviour

3 Changing the *background* can also change behaviour. This can be done by:
   a Removing temptation or
   b Changing the setting or
   c Introducing a prompt.
4 You can also change behaviour by changing the consequences of the behaviour. The main methods of doing this are:
   a Use of selective attention.
   b Reinforcing good behaviour.
   c Sharing responsibility.
   d Time Out.
   e Physical restraint.
5 To change behaviour effectively, always look for the positive.

8

Trouble shooting

Ways to make success in changing behaviour more likely

There is a comment in the Talmud, "The man who seeks for truth is a wise man. The man who thinks he has found it is a fool". When using the functional approach to problem solving it is worth remembering this cautionary line. We have used this approach in countless situations and found it foolproof providing the rules are followed precisely.

Like anything else there are the traps and pitfalls waiting for the unwary, to trip the practitioner up and cause partial or total failure. In this chapter we tell you some of the things that can go wrong and ways of preventing failure.

Monitoring
You may decide to start a programme but for a variety of reasons it never gets started or slips into oblivion before becoming effective.

We avoid this by always setting up a monitoring system for the programme. A monitor is someone who is not at the sharp end operating the programme, but who knows exactly why the programme has been designed, its mechanics and final objectives. The monitor acts as a back-up facility for the operators of the programme and records with them successes and discusses any problems.

Quite clearly if a psychologist, psychiatrist, social worker, doctor or health visitor is helping a parent or teacher deal with a behaviour problem then such a person is the ideal monitor. If on the other hand there is no professional around who can be roped in to help, then the monitor could be another class teacher, a playgroup supervisor, a grandparent or even a trusted neighbour.

The monitor does not have to be involved in the planning and preparation stages. Before the programme starts these should be fully discussed between operator and monitor. The monitor needs to know the framework used to plan the programme and the strategies decided upon. He has to know how the programme will be recorded and the reinforcers or correction procedures to be used. The other bit of vital information required is the length of time the programme is likely to be in force. Given all this information the operator and monitor agree regular meetings spaced at a sensible distance at which report back will occur.

The home teachers on the Wessex Portage project meet their monitor at weekly intervals. They have learned from experience that ten or fifteen minutes is usually a sufficient period of time to discuss one programme. Working with parents and teachers on home-based and school projects we find that between fifteen minutes and half an hour is required per programme for older children.

The monitor can serve other useful functions. Inevitably there are occasions when operators have doubts about a programme or their own behaviour. These doubts could be discussed within families or in staff rooms. Our experience with the approach has taught us that the objectivity of another adult who is not closely involved with the programme helps resolve problems more easily.

The monitor is also a great source of reinforcement for the operator. It is quite lonely working away at changing behaviour and making things better without someone to whom the operator can turn and celebrate successes. Everybody needs someone to notice the good things and a very important part of the monitor's role is back slapping and congratulating and, even having the Kleenex ready if, unfortunately, programmes do not work. In that event (which we have experienced occasionally) the monitor objectively starts ripping into the programme to see what is going wrong.

Mistakes can happen
One programme which went totally wrong was operated in the infant department of a primary school. The subject was a boy called Steven. The teacher successfully ran a programme which reduced his unpleasant habits and increased the behaviour she wanted. Regularly she noticed Steven having little outbursts of bad behaviour. She met her

monitor one Tuesday morning rather depressed with the news that the Head was convinced the programme was a mistake. Analysis of the situation showed that although the teacher was operating her planned programme with great precision, another teacher in the infant department and the dinner ladies were not, although they had been asked to do so. A meeting was held between all those in contact with the child. The teacher explained the success she was having and after quite a stormy debate convinced the others to do exactly the same. Needless to say this had the desired effect and Steven continued to improve. In his case his behaviour had been so bad that at the beginning of the programme the psychologist had begun the paperwork to enable the boy to transfer to a special unit for children described as maladjusted. These events took place four years ago. Happily Steven is now a junior in the primary school, his behaviour is not exemplary but none of the staff perceive him as anything other than high spirited.

This school was so pleased with the success of using a functional approach with Steven that over a period of time they reorganised their disciplinary system. The psychologist for the school has noticed that as the teachers have become more expert at analysing problems and using the functional model, referrals to the school psychologist have decreased.

Generalisation

The monitor can also suggest ways of preventing a second major problem from arising. From time to time school staff, parents and other teachers, notice a child who has learned a new skill or lost an undesirable behaviour, performs perfectly in one situation but cannot produce the same desired behaviour in a slightly different situation.

In other words the child's learning is 'situation specific' and does not transfer or generalise into others. Supposing a mother teaches her child the colours red and blue by always referring to the colour of his jeans or sweater. In such a situation any mother would be pleased when her child apparently learned his colours. She might want to show off his new skill to his father and perhaps says, "Tell Daddy what colour his car is". She is understandably saddened when the child responds with an incorrect answer and obviously has not learned to tell red from blue.

His failure could be because the blue of the car is much paler or darker than his jeans which he has been taught as blue. It could be that

Here we go again!

he has learned blue was an alternative word for jeans and had not related it to colour.

Another example of this kind of specificity is the boy who in school is a little saint and at home resembles Attila the Hun. For such situations we sometimes find that the mother and teacher are using different management techniques and the teacher's strategies are more successful.

Skill generalisation means the child can respond to requests which are similar to but not the same as those he was taught previously. This is known as 'generalisation across behaviours'. Skill generalisation can also mean responding to the same requests in a situation which is different from the one in which the skill was taught. This is known as 'generalisation across settings'.

To teach 'generalisation across behaviours' the answer is to teach the behaviour in a consistent format until firm and then to start gradually introducing slightly different ways of teaching the same behaviour. Teachers are usually extremely clever at making sure children use new learning in a variety of ways. In the case of teaching colour, an infant school teacher might decide to make a red corner in the classroom in which a large number of objects of slightly different reds would be on display. The only common denominator in the corner would be 'redness'. Thus the child would learn to call scarlet or crimson or deep red by the collective name 'red'. He would learn that red was a colour and not an object. The knowledge that the varying shades of red each had their own name would be introduced gradually over several months after the essential feature of 'red' had been established.

In primary schools a large number of materials are usually available to teach basic number work. These might include bricks, rods, counters, an abacus and beads. The teacher can choose to teach any number skill using one set of materials, like bricks and later she can vary the objects used but still teach the same task.

'Generalisation across settings' is usually a matter of using the same or very similar teaching techniques. Supposing a child's teacher is in the habit of ignoring slight misbehaviour, reinforcing good behaviour with attention and providing many interesting activities which keep the child engrossed all day long. Do you think it likely the child would behave in the same way at home if his mother never reinforced good behaviour, picked on him whenever he behaved badly and made few attempts to keep him occupied beyond sitting him in front of the television when he arrived home from school?

In almost all cases where teachers, parents or relations report children acting in different ways in varying settings the fault lies not with the child but with the handling methods of the person concerned. Thus when devising programmes for behavioural change it is sensible, if not essential, for all those in contrast with the child to agree on *their* methods and behaviour. People who complain of Jekyll and Hyde behaviour should start looking at their *own* behaviour before attributing unpleasant characteristics to the child!

Table manners are skills which children have to be taught to apply in a variety of settings. It is not uncommon for parents to be able to tolerate children eating their meals in a sloppy way at home, getting down from the table and running off to play a game as soon as they have begun their last mouthful. Those same parents are sometimes acutely embarrassed when they take their children to tea with friends or to a restaurant and the children do not sit quietly eating. If parents want good table manners in all situations they must maintain standards at home which are the same as those they expect in public places. Table manners have to be taught in different settings if you want them to generalise.

A monitor quite frequently is more sensitive to this problem of generalisation than the people who devised the programme. He is able to point up ways to make sure generalisation occurs.

One of the saddest failures of a programme concerned Bob who at ten years old was 'behaving badly' at home and in school. His mother was divorced and living with a man who had a separated alcoholic wife and two small demanding children. His mother's behaviour fluctuated from deepest love, typified by kisses, presents and blatant spoiling, to total rejection; being sent out of the house, not allowed to sit watching television with the family, refused food and not given any pocket money. The family had attended various Clinics since Bob was two years old and various psychiatrists had 'supported' his mother through her original marriage, three unsuccessful liaisons with other men and the current affair.

The school staff complained that Bob "did nothing right". It was virtually impossible to find a member of staff who had a good word for the boy. The family social worker arranged with the school and the mother for observation to be made in school and home and this led to the construction of a programme. The mother carried out this programme to the letter. This caused some surprise as the social worker had predicted it was unlikely that this mother would be able to be consistent. It was the school staff who did not change *their* behaviour. Bob became good at home but remained unchanged in school.

At this point the psychologist became involved. She recognised that the staff's behaviour towards Bob had become entrenched. There was little chance of a programme succeeding in that school, since the staff could not change their behaviour. Bob was transferred to the school in the next catchment area. Here he was handled consistently and for several months his behaviour was tolerable. At that stage there were further problems at home and his mother reverted to her previous behaviour. Now he was behaving when in school and not at home and also he began truanting.

His behaviour was neither generalising across situations nor being maintained because the adults around him were unable to be consistent. When he truanted it was invariably because his mother failed to get up and give him breakfast and send him to school. On these occasions he would hang around the railings of his old school where the staff would descend on him and chase him away.

His mother may have had many failings but she very much wanted Bob to become a member of her new family and grow up to become a useful adult. Bob similarly wanted an uncomplicated home existence and to conform. The team suggested sending him to a residential school. The psychologist and social worker spent hours analysing the situation and eventually decided this would undoubtedly enable Bob to live in a more structured environment and probably conform to better standards when at home. Both feared, however, that when he returned home he would revert to his old behaviour because the situation there would be unchanged.

An alternative was suggested. The psychologist recommended the child should be taken into care and placed in a children's home where he would be handled consistently and attend the local school which operated a functional approach. Eventually this was organised and Bob's behaviour improved dramatically. His mother is again learning to be consistent with her son. Bob is responding well to the handling he is receiving and generalisation of behaviour across many varied settings is occurring.

This case study demonstrates among other things how difficult it is to get a large group of people to adopt a common plan. Some teachers can become so fixed in their behaviour patterns that it is difficult to arrange a programme to which they will pay more than lip service. In such cases the most sensible course is to help them to plan a programme to change *their* behaviours!

Maintenance

We have discovered one of the most disillusioning aftermaths of a successful programme is when behaviour which has been established and operational for a considerable length of time slowly slides back into that which is not desired. Thus we arrange for most of our programmes to be supported by a maintenance programme.

There are a number of ways of helping a child continue to behave in the new way for a period of time after a programme has ended. It is tempting for parents and teachers after they have altered a child's behaviour to assume everything will now be all right and the child will never revert to former poor standards. It is possible too that people will attribute much of the change to intrinsic child factors rather than the programme.

Almost every successful programme has an element of change in the behaviour of those around the child. Hence if people adopt either of the two approaches quoted above, their own behaviour swiftly returns to pre-programme activity and the inevitable happens, the child follows suit.

One way of preventing such a catastrophe is to continue using the strategy chosen for the programme for a period of time *after* the child has reached the target level for which you aimed. This in the case of new learning of a skill is called *overlearning*.

If the behaviour has been well established and overlearning is not possible, the easiest way to maintain new behaviours is by frequently referring to how pleasing the child's behaviour is when he is carrying out the skill, or not indulging in the disruptive behaviour you have helped him to unlearn. *Pointing up* as this technique is called is made even more effective if carried out in front of other people who matter to the child, like grandparents, special uncles or aunts, or even sisters and brothers.

While new behaviours are being absorbed into a child's repertoire it is likely an artificial form of reinforcer will have been used like a Charley Chart, or stars or even tangibles like sweets, drinks or special rewards. These reinforcers will have been used deliberately and according to a plan. If suddenly they stop and the child who had grown used to an evening session of points counting, or a daily reward or even an instant reward after good behaviour is left high and dry with nothing, it is all a bit too swift and can damage the previous good work. Hence, if, as the time approaches when these reinforcers will no longer be used, the parents begin to phase in other more natural reinforcers like attention, praise, choosing a favourite family meal or arranging a special treat, the child slips from one level of reinforcement to the other and the behaviour continues with no further alteration. Monitors can help parents and teachers to make the change at the best time.

It requires a conscious effort to *phase out artificial reinforcers and phase in natural ones* but these are more effective because they are reinforcers which are more readily available in the real world. If the child is staying with a relation or friend it is fairly simple to explain that special things are happening in the family and would they please notice when the child performs in a certain manner. Would they compliment him in the most natural way if he does play quietly, or eats politely or whatever else the skill or behaviour is that is under scrutiny at that time.

It is effective to involve more people in reinforcing the child's good behaviour. It is wise to inform other people about the strategy being used to teach the new skill or behaviour. Thus all the people who have contact with the child or adult behave in ways which firm up the behaviour more quickly. They all continue to reinforce the child and thus the new behaviour is naturally maintained without the need for further interventions or strategies.

One of the recurrent features of family behaviour is that often a child reacts differently to his mother and father. Mothers report that when alone with their children, they seem to 'get away with blue murder' but behave like angels when their father is present.

We also hear of situations where there is disagreement about handling methods. The child virtually decides to adopt the standards desired by one parent if they appeal to him more than the standards of the other. By involving everyone in behaving in an agreed manner the second of these problems disappear and the first happens less and less often as the child responds to the general structure being imposed.

A monitor can fulfil a useful role in the maintenance stage by arranging for the behaviour to be observed again at regular intervals after the completion of the programme. These recorded observations enable everyone to assess objectively whether the child is behaving in the new way. Initial discussions with a monitor should also cover the pattern of surveillance which will occur at a later date, which will allow progress to be maintained.

A monitor needs to know:

1 How the strategy chosen to change behaviour was chosen.
2 How the strategy is going to operate.
3 How long the strategy is planned to last.
4 How often you want to meet to discuss progress.

A monitor can help you to:

1 Clarify why you wish to change behaviour.
2 Deal with any problems which occur in carrying out the intervention.
3 Celebrate successes which occur during the intervention period.
4 Plan a programme to make sure that the new behaviour continues in other settings (when necessary) by either
   a Introducing slightly different ways of teaching the new behaviour (generalisation across behaviours), or
   b Using the same intervention in a variety of different settings (generalisation across settings).
5 Plan a programme to make sure the child continues the new behaviour after the intervention is completed (maintenance) by either
   a Continuing to use the intervention for a period after the child has reached the desired target level (overlapping), or
   b Frequently praising the new behaviour when it occurs (pointing up), or
   c Chasing in natural reinforcers which are more readily available in the real world.

Just occasionally experts are necessary
Every technique or strategy so far discussed is one which can be operated by any parent or teacher prepared to take the trouble, unaided by an 'expert'. There are several other useful ways of changing behaviour which are a little more complex to learn and others which only an expert can teach. In the first category are such activities as role playing and in the second category complicated skills like relaxation techniques.

Sometimes children, however many times they are told how to behave, just cannot grasp what is required. There are instances of social behaviour, like the way to interrupt someone gracefully, or to accept criticism or correction, or to cope with a crowded party, which some people have difficulty in acquiring. A simple way of teaching such skills is for two or three adults to act out the right way to behave and then invite the child or other adult to play the different roles involved within the group. Taking interruption as an example, two adults might seat themselves in easy chairs and be engrossed in a conversation when a third interrupts. The person trying to learn the skill can observe the effects on the others of different modes of interruption and which is the most socially acceptable and effective. He can then imitate the best behaviour in an acting situation before being given opportunities to practise the skill in many different real world settings.

In such role play activities if a school or family have the good fortune to have access to a video-tape machine the exercise becomes even more successful. The person can witness the other actor's behaviour, participate himself and then see how his behaviour matches up to the model.

Role playing takes a bit of practice and rehearsal before adults can use the technique easily. Not all adults find it comfortable to try to act out a situation. Before involving a child or anyone else in a role play activity it is most essential to have a few dry runs and become word and performance perfect.

Some children and adults have great difficulty in remaining calm when situations begin to get a bit tense. They cannot relax and cope in tricky situations. Such people earn reputations of being irritable, scratchy, bad tempered, unreasonable and many other unpleasant epithets. For some a most useful way of enabling them to cope is to teach them one of the many different relaxation techniques practised today. All of them have to be taught by an expert, none can be just assumed. They cover a wide range of behaviours from meditation through to controlled breathing.

Once a meditation technique or relaxation technique has been learned it can be used to great effect in tense situations. Tennis fans may remember Arthur Ashe meditating in each break during the Wimbledon Men's Singles finals, which he won. Many top sportsmen and women invoke such practices as a form of self-control before major events. There is more than one company chairman of multi-national companies who have learned the same methods to help their equilibrium. Some psychologists can advise on where such techniques can be learned.

This book has offered a structure of clarifying problems, planning how to overcome them and making sure they stay solved, which anyone can use effectively. Stick to the rules and you cannot help being successful. If problems do arise the approach can show you quickly where you went wrong.

All parents and teachers are experts about the people they care for. With a little bit of help in structuring *their* behaviour, we know they deal with most problems supremely well. Good luck!

What we are saying:

1 The system outlined in this book has been successfully used to change behaviour on countless occasions but things can go wrong.
2 A monitor can help you deal with problems as they arise and also celebrate successes with you. Both these functions are vital ones.
3 You may need to plan how to make sure the child can behave as you teach him in different situations.
4 You will possibly have to consider how to make sure the new behaviour is maintained after your successful plan of action has ended.
5 A few methods for changing behaviour are complicated and expert help may be needed in such instances.
6 Parents and teachers are themselves experts about their children.
7 Behaviour can change . . .

References

References which we have found useful:
Burland, J. R. (1979) Behaviour Modification in a Residential School for Junior Maladjusted Boys: A review *Journal of the Association of Workers for Maladjusted Children* Vol. 7, No. 2 Autumn (Chapter 5, page 85).

Cameron, R. J. (1979) A lot can happen at home too *Journal of Remedial Education* November (see Chapter 5, page 68).

Mager, R. F. (1972) *Goal Analysis* Fearon Publishers (see Chapter 2, page 26).

Hedderly, R. (1979) Orange Juice Therapy *Journal of the Association of Educational Psychologists* Vol. 4, No. 9, page 24 (see Chapter 7, page 126).

Skinner, B. F. (1974) *About Behaviourism* Jonathan Cape, London (see Chapter 1, page 5).

Thomas, E. J. and Carter, F. L. (1973) Guidelines for behavioural practice in the open community agency: procedures and evaluation *Journal of Behavioural Research and Therapy* Vol. 2, pages 193–205 (see Chapter 3, page 36).

Advanced Reading:
Becker, W. C. (1971) *Parents are Teachers: A Child Management Programme* Research Press.

Blackham, G. J. and Silberman, A. (1971) *Modification of Child Behavior* Wadsworth Publishing Inc., Belmont, California.

Vargas, J. S. (1977) *Behavioural Psychology for Teachers* Harper and Row.

Glossary

Although we have tried to avoid using technical jargon, inevitably some unfamiliar words have had to be put in. Included in this section is a list of terms which have been used in the book. You do not need to remember the terms, only how to use them to deal directly with problems.

ABC of behaviour: 'A'. stands for 'antecedents', the events which occurred before the behaviour. 'B' is the 'background' or setting in which it took place. 'C' is a reminder to examine the 'consequences' or the effects which the behaviour has caused (Chapter 1, page 5).

Activity Chart: This is a specially designed teaching aid used to teach and record the acquisition of new skills. It was developed as part of the Portage Project (Chapter 5, page 69).

Antecedents: The events which occurred before the behaviour (good or bad) (Chapter 1, page 5).

Background: The setting in which the behaviour (good or bad) took place (Chapter 1, page 5).

Baseline: The performance of the pupil on the first day of teaching is referred to as the 'baseline' (Chapter 5, page 71).

Behaviour: This refers to any clearly describable action. A behaviour can be as slight as a smile or as gross as a temper tantrum! (Chapter 1, page 2).

Behavioural deficits: These are behaviours which occur too rarely or do not occur at all (Chapter 2, page 21).

Behavioural excesses: These are behaviours which occur too frequently and which irritate or annoy others (Chapter 2, page 21).

Charlie Charts: A Charlie Chart is usually a pictorial representation of a child's achievement which can be hung on the wall for all to see (Chapter 5, page 76).

Consequences: These are the events which follow any behaviour (good or bad) (Chapter 1, page 5).

Constant reinforcement: A technical term meaning a behaviour which is reinforced on every occasion it occurs (Chapter 6, page 110).

Contracts: A contract is a signed agreement which states where and how a behaviour will be carried out and what reinforcement will be given. An example is given on page 86 (Chapter 5, page 85).

Correction procedure: This is the procedure used in any teaching situation when a person does not carry out the requested behaviour or carries it out incorrectly (Chapter 5, page 72).

Desired outcome: This is a statement of what people aim for as a result of changed behaviour, i.e. what would be happening if the problem behaviour was overcome or alleviated (Chapter 3, page 36).

Early warning: Using an early warning system can prevent antecedent events from having unpleasant effects. E.g. telling children that bedtime will occur twenty minutes later (Chapter 7, page 115).

Extinguished: When a behaviour no longer occurs, it is described as 'extinguished' (Chapter 7, page 130).

Formal teaching: This expression is used to describe a planned and evaluated teaching session or programme (Chapter 5, page 62).

Functional approach: In a functional or behavioural approach to problem behaviours the functions of antecedent, background and consequent result are examined (Chapter 1, page 6).

Fuzzies: Fuzzies are unclear, imprecise and frequently ambiguous statements used to describe behaviours (Chapter 2, page 26).

Generalisation across skills: Responding to requests which are similar to but not the same as those taught (Chapter 8, page 137).

Generalisation across settings: Responding to the same request in a setting different from the one in which the skill was taught (Chapter 8, page 137).

Informal teaching: Teaching which occurs naturally without analysing the situation beforehand or identifying which skills to teach (Chapter 5, page 62).

Intermittent reinforcement: The technical description of when behaviours are reinforced either occasionally or randomly (say five times out of a possible twenty occasions) (Chapter 6, page 110).

Long-term targets or goals: A long-term target is one which will be attained, not after a week or after a month, but after several months or even years (Chapter 4, page 49).

Maintenance schedule: This is the smallest or lowest possible level of reinforcement which is required to hold a child's behaviour at a desired level (Chapter 6, page 110).

Modelling: Showing the person being taught how to do a behaviour correctly (Chapter 5, page 72).

Monitor: A Monitor is a person who acts as a back-up facility, with whom parents and teachers record successes and discuss problems (Chapter 8, page 133).

Monitoring: An agreed and actioned plan for discussing a programme with a Monitor (Chapter 8, page 133).

Negative statements list: Part of a priority problem list relating directly to those behaviours which people would most like to change (Chapter 3, page 36).

Overlearning: Continuing to practise a new behaviour for a period after the person has attained the target aimed at (Chapter 8, page 140).

Performances: A description of a problem behaviour which is made clear in precise and non-ambiguous terms (Chapter 2, page 26).

Physical guidance: Holding on to a child and guiding his limbs through an activity (Chapter 5, page 72).

Physical restraint: Holding on to a child in a manner which is neither aggressive nor unpleasant but still enables him to regain control of himself (Chapter 7, page 130).

Pointing up: Frequently telling or showing a person being taught that you are pleased that he is continuing to carry out the desired behaviour (Chapter 8, page 140).

Portage project: This is a home visiting scheme for families with a handicapped pre-school child (Chapter 5, page 68).

Positive behaviour assets: This part of a P.P.L. lists at least three statements about the person concerned which illustrate positive behaviours (Chapter 3, page 36).

Post-baseline: The results on the day on which the child should have achieved the skill are referred to as 'post-baseline' performance (Chapter 5, page 71).

Priority problem: This is the most pressing or urgent problem on the problem list (Chapter 3, page 36).

Priority problem list: There are four elements to a P.P.L.:

a positive statements.

b statements describing behaviour deficits and excesses.

c an agreed priority problem.

d the desired outcome of successfully treating the priority problem (Chapter 3, page 36).

Reinforcement: This refers to any event which when it follows a behaviour will make it more likely that the behaviour will occur again (Chapter 6, page 108).

Selective attention: Responding selectively to a behaviour means either reinforcing or ignoring that behaviour when it occurs. Attending to a behaviour is likely to lead to an increase in frequency, ignoring it will usually decrease the frequency of the behaviour in question (Chapter 7, page 119).

Success procedure: A success procedure makes it clear to a child that he has successfully completed a behaviour or attained a teaching target (Chapter 5, page 71).

Success rate: This is the degree of success which you would like to see being attained after teaching a new skill for an agreed period of time (Chapter 5, page 69).

Task analysis: The process used to break down a long-term target behaviour into a number of smaller easy steps or stages (Chapter 4, page 50).

Time Out: Taking the child away from a difficult situation and placing him on his own in a quiet area, leaving him for not longer than ten minutes. This gives him Time Out from the unpleasant experiences and a chance to calm down (Chapter 7, page 127).

Teaching target or target behaviour: This is the behaviour which parents and/or teachers would like to see the child attaining at the end of an agreed period of time, say one week (Chapter 5, page 69).

Verbal correction: Telling a child where he or she went wrong and asking him or her to begin again (Chapter 5, page 72).